VERY**MUCH**WOW

I have more respect for somebody who points at his ideal — in this case, the ideal of the pirate — and then becomes something that's more radical, more exciting, more subversive than a pirate could ever be.

—Will Oldham

VERYMUCHWOW
WWW.VERYMUCHWOW.COM
BIRDIE JAWORSKI
EDITOR

Donations help keep VERY MUCH WOW alive!

Our Dogecoin Address is:
DQmDQT2GoqVZmXb18w27HS6oZecpf9p3Sa

All contributors, columnists, and artists
are paid in Dogecoin
for their submissions to VERY MUCH WOW.

Want to write for VMW?
Have art to share with VMW's audience?

Please contact:
editor@verymuchwow.com

ARTWORK CREDITS

*All artwork in Very Much Wow is created
by the artists credited beneath each piece.
Other pieces are copyright Very Much Wow.*

SHIBES LOVE FEEDBACK

info@verymuchwow.com

Published by:

VERY MUCH WOW
Albuquerque, New Mexico, USA
T 505 216 6187

You can measure the depth of Dogecoin's life experiences with the same 7 to 1 ratio in which its namesake measures its years. We've fit an incredible amount of mining, tipping, donating, buying, developing, building, helping, exasperating, proselytizing, and drama into these past few months. Whether you believe Dogecoin is a viable currency or not, you have to admit that the community and its coin have indelibly changed the digital money landscape.

Cryptocurrency hijacked the financial world with a Jolly Roger in the shape of a gold circle with a barred "B." As much as we like to think that our little coin has changed the world, Bitcoin did it first, did it bigger, did it with more lasting financial consequences. Despite its prowess on the racetrack, Dogecoin isn't making bankers quake in their tasseled loafers, and try as they might, unscrupulous shibes can't con the community out of more than our tiny market cap. Bitcoin carries the sword. We carry a squirt gun.

Every crypto coin is a tool for subversion and beauty, sometimes at the same time. The technology combines ultimate transparency with absolute anonymity. There is no more perfect and terrifying a promise. The mantra heard throughout the cryptocurrency world is "trust no one." The consensus algorithm doesn't care for your age, your looks, your ideas. It cares only that its independent nodes agree on the flow of electron.

"Trust no one" only describes the reliability of the technical transaction itself. It is the center movement in a concerto. The first and final movements, however, require both trust and confidence. Cryptocurrency still involves relationships between people. We haven't yet coded our DNA out of the entire system.

When you make a purchase, you trust the merchant to provide you with a good or service. You must have confidence that the merchant can follow through on her promise. You may

there be rough seas, and we are but lost doges

trust that a person is good and has wonderful intentions, but you may lack the confidence in their ability to follow through on their promise.

Cryptocurrency involves the belief that the people on both sides of the algorithm are willing and committed. There is no "trust no one" in reality. There is only "I want to believe." Even in straight financial transactions, you still must establish a level of trust and confidence in the company, organization, or website in which you place your Doge.

The other part of the promise - anonymity - is also problematic. Being anonymous is a good thing if you feel you are in danger, if you think that someone is out to get you. But desiring anonymity is always a reaction to threat: fear of government, of thieves, of exposing your own frailties. A society based on anonymity is not the basis of a pleasant or healthy culture. If no one has to have a relationship with anyone else, I would call that society ill.

If anonymity is seen as a legitimate alternative to transparency, it paradoxically paints you as "can't be trusted." In place of transparency, the result is like obfuscation. Anonymity is not a neutral position. It is the absence of disclosure. This is great if there is nothing at stake, but you cannot build community on what is hidden. We're a conflicted people in this regard. We abhor our government's reach into our private lives, yet we line up for Google Glass and scour the internet for evidence of our neighbor's lifestyle.

For all of human history, we have built relationships with the people in whom we do business. We began by bartering, not only because we needed goods that others had, but because we desired the cultural interaction. Historically, marketplaces have been some of our most valuable cultural centers. People would cross the high desert here in New Mexico in order to attend the yearly market in Santa Fe. The meeting of others was as important as the goods one would trade and receive. People discussed the weather, waring tribes, peace treaties, the buffalo herds, and shared ideas about the nature of their community and world. Thousands of years before and miles away, the Greeks met in the Agoras to trade but also to discuss the world, philosophy, and politics.

Humans have never wanted pure transactions. They want added value. They want to adorn their belongings, to forge an identity. We don't wear plain clothing and drive simple boxes with wheels. We find

styles that we like, we make beautiful recipes that both taste and look good instead of simply nourish us with calorie and macronutrient. Everything that humans do, want, touch, is centered in ideas of culture and community. Even when humans were piling rocks together, they didn't build a rugged algorithm that did what it needed to do and nothing else; they built monuments and statues and great works of lasting art.

When currencies were developed, they became emissaries of those cultures; the pictures and emblems and phrases on paper currency hold meaning to those in the community, and makes a statement. The symbols didn't make the currency reliable, but it connected the user to her world.

Dogecoin is a currency build around ideas of community, trust, and confidence. We are not a faceless blockchain. We wear the face of a dog. The blockchain itself may require no trust, but the Shibe on either end requires it. You can have confidence that the consensus algorithm will always be verified. But you need trust and confidence in the community in order for Dogecoin to succeed.

None of these added values could be there if everything was hidden and anonymous, in fact, they depend on transparency and knowledge of who and what is involved. I like to think that Dogecoin is the ultimate tool of transparency: we open up our transactions to scrutiny in the blockchain, and by forging real relationships with others in our community, we open up our lives and trust to them as well. We may never have the marketcap of Bitcoin, but we may be the little coin that changes the ways in which people begin to combine community with commerce with real transparency, with trust and confidence. In other words: Verify. But Trust.

When we look over our human history, our need to share story and decorated good, we realize that we have always lives in a world of serious, funny, beautiful, artistic, and crazy memes. Who in the world doesn't like looking at a nice dog? Which kind of cryptocurrency, then, is in our future?

Unless the entire history of humanity means nothing, it's got a damned dog on it, and it's going to be on the moon, too.

Birdie

Thank you, /u/TakerOne for my beautiful and comfy Dogeshirt!

JYRO BLADE

Jyro is a video game programmer working in the New York City indie game development scene. He has been making games since he was 14. He became involved with Doge in February 2014. Jyro enjoys DJing UK hardcore, skateboarding, and playing competitive Magic: The Gathering.

jyro@verymuchwow.com

CLAY M. GILLESPIE

Clay is an amateur writer of novels, short stories, poems and comic book scripts. He has created and implemented strategic plans for Goodwill Industries, Asian American Alliance of Indiana, Martin Luther King Jr. Dream Team, Digital Publishing Studios and Ball State University's Unified Student Media.

clay@verymuchwow.com

CARLISHIO2

Carlishio2 is a coder aspiring to become a comic book artist. He lives in Puerto Vallarta. Not too long ago he had an idea for a comic based on Dogecoin.

You can find his work at dogecoinball.com

carlishio2@verymuchwow.com

ROSS NICOLL

Ross Nicoll is one of the core developers for Dogecoin.

See Ross' column for information on how you can help support our Dogecoin developers.

FREE1000

Free1000 built his first computer in 1985. That's how long he's been in the computer business. He owns a Finance company and VR Concepts, a Virtual Reality Computer company that's been around since 1993. Originally from Seattle, he lives in New Jersey with his wife and four children.

Free1000@verymuchwow.com

TIM BOLBROCK

Tim was born in the suburbs of New York City and began programming as a child. He graduated from Cooper Union and was a research assistant at Penn State before returning to NYC to work as a software developer. Dogecoin got him to jump into coins and currently he is a board member of Very Charity, Inc.

VMW COLUMNISTS

DR. LOW DOG

Dr. Anthony Low is a physicist and theorist. He was born, raised and currently resides in New York City. His passion for dogs, technology, community development, and cultural disruption are confluent in his unbridled enthusiasm for Dogecoin.

lowdogtheory@verymuchwow.com

TOM BOICE

Tom Boice is a regular contributor to the cryptocurrency news service CryptoCoinsNews.com, spearheading their weekly Dogecoin addition. Holding a B.A. in English Literature from the University of West Florida, Tom has a passion for all things music and loves analyzing song composition.

tom@verymuchwow.com

VERY MUCH DR BOB

Very Much Doctor Bob, Professor of Shibemetrics, analyzes the Dogecoin community from a variety of interesting and doge-like angles.

verymuchdoctorbob
@verymuchwow.com

EDGAR BOUNDS

Edgar once bought $10 dollar time-travel voucher service that claimed to deposit $9 of the $10 dollars in a fund to accumulate over the millennia, turning into a fortune that will be used when time-travel becomes viable to go back in time and rescue him.

edgar@verymuchwow.com

GOOD SHIBE

GoodShibe is a passionate advocate for Dogecoin, a regular contributor to the /r/Dogecoin community and writer of the popular 'Of Wolves and Weasels' series – an archive of which can be found at goodshibe.com.

goodshibe@verymuchwow.com

HELEN ENSIKAT

Helen is a small-time doge holder from Western Australia with a background in economics and corporate finance. This one time she saw an advertisement for a Very Much Wow columnist, and thought 'Wow, what a career opportunity!'

helen@verymuchwow.com

SUCH INFO

The World Of CRYPTOCURRENCY

DARKCOIN

VERTCO

LESSER ALTS ISLES

BLOCKCHAIN SEA

PEERCOIN

SO TABLE MUCH CONTENTS

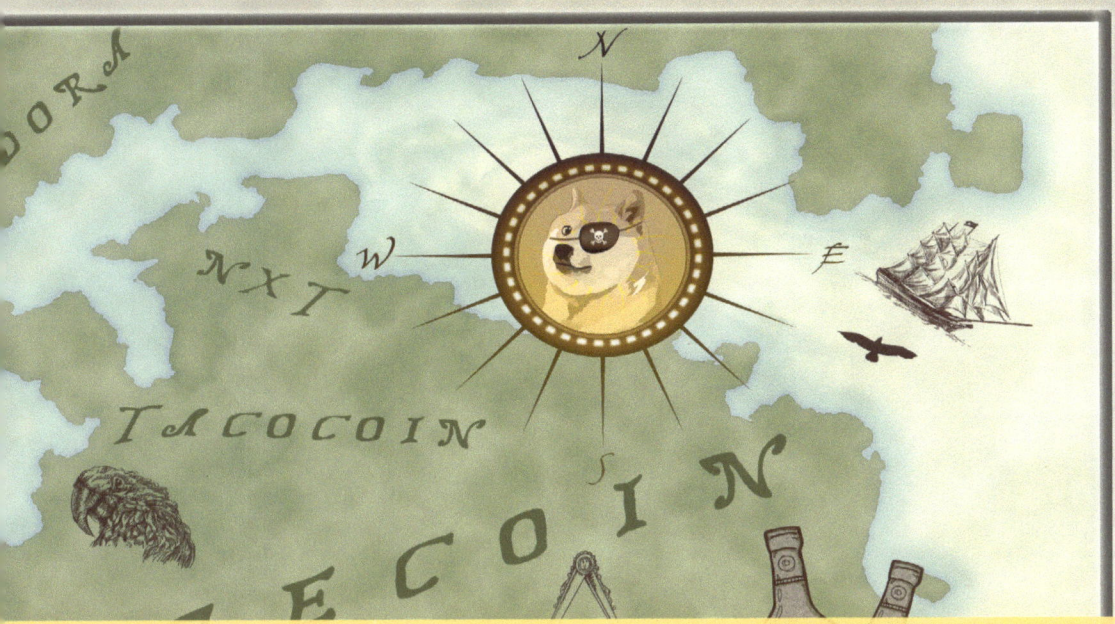

NEWS BRIEFS

Josh Wise

*Chris Higgins (left) and Adam Cornelius
pose while filming "Coined"
Josh Wise (above) during his "Coined interview*

"Coined" Documentary Launches Kickstarter Campaign

Money is changing. With the launch of Bitcoin in 2009, traditional notions of currency changed forever, expanding to include a digital, community-driven monetary system known as cryptocurrency. Since Bitcoin's inception, new cryptocurrencies such as Dogecoin are created each month with unique agendas, technical advancements, and varying personalities.

Because monetary systems are shifting so rapidly, there is an urgent need to critically explore this transformation and document history before it is lost. Award-winning director Adam Cornelius and This American Life contributor Chris Higgins have joined forces to produce Coined, the first ever feature-length documentary to focus on altcoins, the lesser-known cousins of Bitcoin.

The film will shed light on the stories of those who embraced Bitcoin technology and took it to the next level: those who invented new coins, built businesses around them, and created communities to support each other. Since they began filming in January 2014 Cornelius and Higgins have shot over 20 hours, with

significant coverage of Dogecoin, a meme-based cryptocurrency that surged in popularity and value since its creation in December 2013.

Existing footage includes:
- First-ever on-camera interviews with Dogecoin creator Billy Markus
- Exclusive footage of the "Dogecar"—a Dogecoin-sponsored race car—and interviews with NASCAR driver Josh Wise
- Interviews with Josh Mohland, creator of the Dogecoin tipbot
- The first "Dogeparty" on Wall Street in New York City
- Interviews with cryptocurrency activists, economists, and business owners who accept Bitcoin and Dogecoin

To finance additional filming of new digital currency stories as they develop, the duo has launched a Kickstarter campaign. The campaign ends on July 16th, 2014, with a funding goal of $72,000. Kickstarter backers will receive behind-the-scenes updates about the film during production and rewards options include digital downloads of the film, DVDs, the film's soundtrack, and even producer credits.

Dogecoin Foundation V 2.0 Forms

After extensive discussions and consultations, there is finally, on the table, a legally formed Dogecoin Foundation, which will be populated my members in the coming weeks. Everyone understood from the start it would not be easy, but now it has been completed and the Dogecoin community has access to a respectable and organized structure.

For the last few weeks the team putting this all into place have been working tremendously hard behind the scenes to identify the correct approach to implementation, thereby making sure that the new foundation will possess the capabilities to deliver all that Dogecoin needs as both a currency and a community.

Interested parties can currently make their views known via posts on discuss.dogecoin.com (the Official Dogecoin forum) and on reddit.com/r/dogecoin.

SuchList.com Adds New Features

SuchList.com, a buying and selling platform using Dogecoin, had added new features to its popular site. Users may now search for Dogecoin offers by location. Shibes may select their offers to be available World Wide, on specific continents, in specific countries, and in specific regions within countries or specific cities within a country - all by way of an easy-to-use hierarchical tree.

In addition, the site has implemented a comprehensive new buyer and seller feedback system.

Social Network Tipping Service Launches

Cryptiv.com has launched, offering its users the ability to send digital currencies on a variety of social media networks from one simple wallet.

Users can check their balance, see when and who sent them coins, and tip any of their friends and followers on their favorite social media sites. Cryptiv.com is a multi-currency platform that currently supports both Bitcoin and Dogecoin.

VoidSpace: Gaming With Dogecoin

Universeprojects.com has opened a Kickstarter for their new twitch-based MMORPG. Set set in a sandboxed world called The Void, the multi-platform game offers players the ability to create their own infrastructure to survive.

VoidSpace promises users the ability to use Dogecoin as in-game currency.

GOT NEWS?
email editor@verymuchwow.com
with your news tips, press releases,
photographs, and Dogecoin gossip!

DOGE SHOOTS FOR 'DEGA

It is a strange phenomenon, the internet. It has the ability to take a mere concept and explode into things that were once nearly unimaginable. Over the span of the last six months, a brilliant example of this occurrence is the advent of the Dogecoin community. Dogecoin is a digital cryptocurrency similar in form and function to other cryptocurrencies such as Bitcoin and Litecoin. A cryptocurrency, in nature, is a strange technological breakthrough. The currency exists only as data spread across many computers, and its value is limited only by its uses. Being entirely decentralized, the currency relies on the community to shape its future.

With the emergence of Dogecoin, a new form of community has taken hold. Rather than a community that seeks only to increase the value of its individual coins, for their own personal gain, the community strives to assist those around them by conquering any obstacle that stands within their way. And the community has done great things for a vast array of different charities, groups, and people. Some of which include sending the Jamaican bobsled team to the Sochi Olympics, building fresh water wells in Kenya, and even sponsoring NASCAR driver Josh Wise to allow him to race at Talladega.

Dogecoin's involvement with Josh Wise continues to be one of their largest undertakings and has spawned a plethora of new community members, lovingly referred to as Shibes (named after their mascot, the Shiba Inu). In total, the Dogecoin community has donated in excess of $100,000 USD toward Josh Wise and Phil Parsons Racing (the team to which Josh belongs). The original $50,000 was raised strictly by the community through a "charity drive" of sorts, with everyone pitching in as much as they feasibly could.

However, due to the newfound massive popularity of Josh Wise and Dogecoin, through collaboration with Phil Parsons, the community was able to raise another $50,000+ by selling an official DogeCrew T-Shirt, of which, over 6,500 were ordered! Thanks to this massive fundraiser, the community was able to fund another race at Talladega for Josh.

Nonetheless, the community now has a new objective that they are striving for in their ongoing saga with NASCAR. There is currently a massive undertaking for the community to fund the presence of a sponsorship tent at this year's October Talladega SuperSpeedway race. The team in charge of running the event is hoping to raise in excess of $17,000, which will be used to pay the booth rental, as well as order a large plethora of items in which to giveaway to curious NASCAR fans. The team's goal is to demonstrate what the Dogecoin community is, and what exactly we do.

So be on the lookout for the Doge4Dega DogeHat fundraiser so you can help spread the word of Dogecoin, and allow our community to grow.

To the Moon,
JD Davis

Donate to Doge4Dega:
DEGA4PRNL5qY1vSKXK5pdvetdRq9DHbKQr

Josh Wise Dogecar photographs courtesy of Doge4Dega's /u/ PM_ME_YOUR_TITS_GIRL

DOGECOIN 101

DOGE ON A CHAIN

Perhaps, late at night, you wonder "How does Dogecoin actually work?" This article will hopefully answer your question.

If you're this deep into a Dogecoin magazine, you most likely already know how Dogecoin works in use; you have a wallet and simply receive with your wallet address and send to another wallet address. That's the important part for you. Under the hood though, Dogecoin uses the breakthrough "blockchain" technology introduced by Bitcoin. Digital currencies like Dogecoin and Bitcoin use the blockchain to maintain a public ledger of coins, a permanent record of every transaction ever made with that particular currency.

PUBLIC KEY CRYPTOGRAPHY

Cryptography is the study and implementation of secure communications in a hostile environment like the Internet. Secrets and passwords used to encode and decode are called "keys" and "public key cryptography" uses keys that come in pairs. The private key is secret, and the public key is shared with whom you would like to communicate.

Crypto Currencies use "digital signatures" that are generated by signing a message with the private key. The signature is a chunk of data that can be decoded with the public key, proving the generator of that message knew the private key. The private key always remains secret. The transaction algorithm only verifies the message was signed with the right private key and does not determine whether the public (receiving) key belongs to the right person.

These "private keys" are the same Dogecoin private keys you have locked inside your digital wallet file or written on your paper wallet. "Public address" is pretty close to "public key" and addresses are just shortened versions of public keys. You could look at public addresses as numbered Dogecoin accounts.

Knowing a Dogecoin private key allows you to sign a transaction message. This message transfers DOGE from your public address to the destination public address, and the digital signature verifies you have the right to send the DOGE, but keeps the private key secret. Transaction messages are broadcast to the entire Dogecoin peer-to-peer network, passed around until everyone has a copy - you will know this process as "verification."

One way to understand it - private keys are your passwords that allow you to send DOGE from your associated numbered account.

THE DOUBLE SPEND

So, public key cryptography allows you to prove an address is yours and spend the currency, but blocks others because they don't have your private key. You do this by signing transaction messages. Cryptography, however, considers the potential for hostile "adversaries" exploiting weaknesses in the system with "attacks."

One attack is the Double Spend. Signed transaction messages mean only one party can spend from a given address, but that one party can cheat. This can happen when an attacker sends a properly signed transaction from a smartphone to a merchant to buy an expensive item. At the same time, the attacker has servers elsewhere send out a properly signed transaction moving the same digital currency to another address they control. The scam is that the merchant initially sees the transaction where an item is paid for but in the end the other transaction may win out. The bad guy could keep both product and currency, and the merchant gets nothing.

BLOCKS IN A CHAIN

The pseudonymous Satoshi Nakomoto overcame this obstacle with the Bitcoin blockchain and the mining protocol that supports it. Coin network users can participate in the mining process, verifying transactions and earning block rewards and transaction fees in return for spending on hardware and power. Miners receive transaction messages from the peer-to-peer network and process them as follows...

Each miner checks transactions for validity and makes sure they are consistent, that is, no attempts to spend the same coins twice! They try to sign these transactions as a "block" which basically is composed of:

- a link to the previous block - thus the block "chain"
- all unconfirmed transactions the miner has received
- a special transaction paying the miner's rewards

- an arbitrary number called a *"nonce"*

During this signing process, a random number called a "hash" is generated - these are usually written in hexadecimal form, meaning the digits are 0-9 then A-F. This number is unpredictable but can be repeatedly produced from the same input data.

By trying different nonces, miners can compute thousands or millions of hashes a second. As I write, the DOGE network computes over fifty billion hashes a second. Depending on the level of difficulty, hashes below a certain number are considered winners. A winning "block" is published to the blockchain and the transactions in it receive one confirmation. Other miners, network nodes, and users accept blocks that follow the protocol's rules. These form the public ledger - the blockchain.

So each hash computation is essentially like a lottery ticket, and miners compete by trying more hashes. They make sure everything is consistent and seal transactions behind ever-increasing numbers of confirmations.

To double spend, a hostile party needs to solve more blocks than the rest of the network (to rewrite history, in order to keep their coin), requiring near impossible amounts of luck or an incredible amount of computing power.

Of course, that leaves out a great amount of detail, but part of Dogecoin's message is that it's not necessary to read this column before use. Future articles will look more closely at different aspects, issues, and questions - such as "what is a dogecoin, really?"

Tip Tom:
DLDxcJgYUYjKyYMtffs4k8KMxEBUqrhwrg

Bitcoin entrepreneur Andreas Antonopoulos has founded several Bitcoin businesses as well as launched several community open-source projects. He serves as the Chief Security Officer of Blockchain.

Andreas spoke with *Very Much Wow* about the future of cryptocurrencies, and what lessons Dogecoin has taught Bitcoin and other cryptocurrencies.

VMW: On the role and the future of cryptocurrencies - have your thoughts changed over time?

AA: They have changed quite a bit. I used to think there was room for a handful of currencies. I thought that through competition we would see many failed attempts, but in essence would only see four or five cryptocurrencies that would emerge. I've revised my opinion on that. I've started looking at it from a different perspective.

Currency is a form of expression and a component for social interaction. In fact, it is a behavior that is emergent among social species, not just humans.

Primates develop currencies, for example. If you observe primary school children, in the absence of currency they create currency in order to interact socially - whether through trading rubber bands or lollypops or Pokemon cards.

This is not a new behavior. This is a behavior that is hundreds of millennia old. You have a bunch of hairy proto-humans who are socially interacting; before long, they are going to start exchanging shells, beads, feathers, and other things that act as abstractions of value. These things don't have intrinsic value.

That's the key to understanding the difference between currency and barter. With barter you exchange things that have intrinsic value, such as fruit or water. When you move to a level of abstraction, when you begin exchanging things that have no intrinsic value, you begin using those tokens - beads, feathers - in a language.

Once you look at it from that perspective, the question about how many alt-coins there will be is equivalent to the question of how many bloggers there

will be on the Internet. Once you break the link between a fixed market for these things - like we've had with publishing institutions or financial institutions - you allow anyone to use those as a tool of expression, and in response, people will start using them.

It's rapidly getting to the point where using web script or websites developed for this purpose, a primary schoolchild will be able to create a fully-fledged cryptocurrency with monetary policy, mining algorithm, etc. That's essentially just a better Pokemon card. I've nicknamed that "Joeycoin" to compete with "Mariacoin." As bizarre as that seems, I think it is inevitable.

VMW: How many cryptocurrencies do you think there will be in the future, and how will their values be established?

AA: We have to start thinking about valuable cryptocurrencies versus non-valuable cryptocurrencies. We have to examine the idea of where value comes from and how we establish value in a currency. In the past, value in a currency was determined by the issuer in a top-down fashion. Sovereignty creates value through scarcity. A monopoly of issuance is what gives a currency its value.

In the world we live in now, currencies acquire value because of use. The user base you have for adoption determines whether it is valuable or not. Your ability to use it in a broad environment, or in a narrow environment that you care about also determines value. If you can use your coin to do commerce in a broad setting, then it will hold monetary value.

But monetary value isn't the only value. Social value is another concern. Even narrow social value. Joeycoin has value to Joey and his friends. It doesn't have monetary value, not even to Joey, but it has value.

VMW: How does social value and monetary value happen?

AA: You might start with something that has social value, and then it gradually gains monetary value through sheer volume of adoption. Dogecoin is a good example. You start off with a joke and a meme and then it becomes a currency.

Imagine - ten years from now - a village in Africa and they have two currencies: one denominated in pounds sterling or some equivalent that has a picture of the

British queen on it and one denominated in Dogecoin that has the picture of the dog on it. To the residents of that village, both are bizarre. They have no clue who this white lady is and why she is on their money, and they have no clue who this dog is and why it's on their money. The only question then is, "can you buy six eggs with it?"

VMW: How can cryptocurrencies move into the developing world - especially into places with limited technological access?

AA: I think, eventually, it's inevitable. Cryptocurrencies allow countries to leapfrog directly to a monetary system that has few overheads, one that is less costly. It immediately opens up the global markets.

If there is a gap in technology, you are going to see more availability of feature phones and SMS gateways. At the same time, we are seeing that smart phones are getting cheaper and cheaper. We're starting to see twenty-five dollar Android phones. Now, twenty-five dollars may be a large amount to pay today in Sub-Saharan Africa, but if you imagine one person investing in that phone and turning it into a Bloomberg terminal, a Western Union terminal that can do lending, banking, wireless transactions and remittances for the entire village, twenty-five dollars is a reasonable investment.

Andreas Antonopoulos

Cell phones travel much faster than other technologies because they have significant and immediate impacts on the lives of people. You see villages where they have no electricity, cook with wood fires, have no running water, and you see a one-foot square solar panel on the roof of a mud hut. The only reason that it's there is to charge their Nokia feature phone because that's their link to the rest of the world.

Where there is a need, and the solutions become just barely affordable, they spread as wildfire. Landlines never took off in Africa because the costs were too high, yet mobile phones have spread very quickly, and in this same manner, cryptocurrencies will replace traditional banking.

There is no way that the Central Bank of Nigeria can build branches to serve all of their rural population. In central Brazil, 75% of the population is unbanked. It's not because they don't have money, and they don't have commerce. It's because the cost of infrastructure is too high. These banks are very interested in Bitcoin as a way to deliver secure banking through SMS.

VMW: Do cryptocurrencies need to remain open-source?

AA: The whole point of cryptocurrencies is "trust no one." I think we've seen already with Ripple that proprietary cryptocurrencies do not work. Open-source and cryptocurrencies are a very natural fit. They leverage the same community decentralized spirit.

Quite honestly I don't think there's room for proprietary software in general, not just cryptocurrencies. Almost everything is gradually becoming open-source. Proprietary software rots faster. It's impossible for companies to maintain software in a proprietary format; it is inefficient.

VMW: Governments across the world have issues with cryptocurrency. They don't understand it. They are unsure how to deal with it. Do you see this becoming an increasing problem or a decreasing problem?

AA: I think it depends on the country. More liberal countries with a vibrant middle class, high levels of education and literacy, freedoms and civil liberties will embrace cryptocurrency like they embrace the internet. But countries where they have no respect for human rights, where there is a massive imbalance in rights, powers, freedoms, and wealth, where a tiny minority controls government, they will see cryptocurrencies as threatening in exactly the same way as they see the internet as threatening.

We will see flailing and bad attempts to ban cryptocurrency. In the end, all that does is reveal their level of despair and desperation.

You can't ban global cryptocurrencies. You can't uninvent the consensus algorithm system, the invention of Satoshi Nakamoto, the blockchain with proof of work. That invention has happened. You can no longer uninvent that like you cannot uninvent electricity or thermodynamics.

When you have fragmentation and isolation in the natural world, it causes evolution to accelerate. If you take a country like Russia and they decide to ban Bitcoin, you will see the evolution of highly stealthy and uniquely Russian coins that are uniquely suited to bribery and corruption of the Russian system, diverting the Russian legal system, and subverting the authoritarian rule. Those versions of cryptocurrency will be much better suited for the Russian environment, and will evolve to be much more dynamic for that niche, rights, powers, freedom, and wealth. The more authoritarian the government is, the more radical the coins.

In terms of cryptocurrencies, Bitcoin is a cuddly little Panda bear.

VMW: What is the future of Bitcoin? Will it go the distance, or eventually be replaced by something else?

AA: I think Bitcoin is going to go the distance because its fundamental network effect makes it very well suited for a specific niche, the long-term store of value coin that provides the backbone for a very solid, low volatility value. You can't see that now. But in the long term, I think that Bitcoin will be far more stable than gold, far more stable than any national currency, and will be used to back other cryptocurrencies, national currencies, sovereign debts, and many other transactions and activities.

Bitcoin won't necessarily be the shopping coin. It won't necessarily be the day-to-day transaction coin. It will be the coin you invest for your retirement. It will be the twenty year, not the twenty day coin.

There is room for many, many coins. I don't see any of the alt-coins as threatening to Bitcoin. Their adoption feeds into Bitcoin's power and value and makes Bitcoin more robust. Bitcoin becomes the reserve currency for all of the other coins. Altcoins validate the core premise of cryptocurrency by expanding it into more and more niches.

We are going to be living in a world full of cryptocurrencies, perhaps thousands, perhaps hundreds of thousands or millions, many of which we will never see - they will be behind the scenes. These cryptocurrencies will allocate and relocate bandwidth, will act as currency in exchange between machine systems and automated systems. Your electricity meter will talk to your electricity company with its own cryptocurrency, your car will talk to your leasing company using its own cryptocurrency, and most of the time you won't even see these things happen.

I think we're in for a world in which the core consensus algorithm will define thousands of niches where it can be applied, and out of that it will spawn types of currencies that will fill those niches.

VMW: Any thoughts on Dogecoin?

AA: Dogecoin proved a couple of things. It proved that you can easily cross the chasm from meme to monetary value. In the future it may prove that you can cross back and lose monetary value and turn back into a fad. We don't know. Dogecoin is still an experiment.

Dogecoin also shows that you can attract a very different demographic. Bitcoin is very serious; it's quite political at least in terms of its early adopters. And in terms of those early adopters it had a purist culture behind it.

And Dogecoin doesn't have those same principles. It has googly eyes and "wow." The less serious nature of Dogecoin appeals to a broader demographic, and that is a very important lesson for Bitcoin and other cryptocurrencies, too.

I think it's great. It shows that the concept of an unforgeable, provably fair trusted system can fill any niche, and can work in any social environment, and has broad appeal. If anybody ever said that cryptocurrencies are only for Libertarian nerds, all you have to do is point to Dogecoin.

> "If anybody ever said that cryptocurrencies are only for Libertarian nerds, all you have to do is point to Dogecoin."

HEATERS GONNA HEAT

FREE1000
THE NEW GOLD RUSH

So you want to mine crypto-currency. You've come to the right place to get information. Maybe you're new to alt-coins, so those of you, who already mine, bear with us for a minute. We need a quick refresher for the new miner, then right into the "meat & potatoes" for the rest of us.

Mining virtual currency is being called "the new gold rush." What is mining, you may ask. You are using your computer's CPU or GPU (Graphics Card) to crunch numbers.

All virtual currencies are a complex algorithm. Your computer solves these algorithms online and stores them on a network called a blockchain . A blockchain is an online ledger that stores all of these transactions. When you or a group of people solve a block, you are rewarded with virtual coins. When a group of people join their computing power together to mine, this is called a mining "pool." I will predominately be talking about Đogecoin mining, but I will give a quick rundown of the different types of coins and how they are mined.

First there were sha-256 coins, the Grandfather being Bitcoin. Five years ago you could mine Bitcoin with your computer. As the Bitcoin network grew, it became impossible to make money mining with graphics cards. Then ASIC's came out, or Application-Specific Integrated Circuits. These were very expensive at first, but they were way more energy efficient than graphics cards. They were made to mine much faster.

Then scrypt coins came out, like our father Litecoin. Scrypt coins were made to prevent ASIC's from mining up all the coins. Scrypt coins were mined by CPU's and GPU's for a few years. Now recently, ASIC's for mining scrypt coins have come onto the market. The cycle is starting to repeat itself from what happened in the Bitcoin market. This is where something called "difficulty" comes into play. When more power or "hashrate" is on a network, the difficulty of mining automatically increases. This makes it harder to mine coins. As the networks grow, the difficulty goes up, so more and more hashrate is required to mine the same amount of coins.

Many new coins have come out with different parameters built in to make them only mineable by graphics cards. Scrypt-N and X-11 have become the two most popular new coin algorithms. Mining with GPU's is to the point where you will never get your ROI (Return On Investment) back. Small Scrypt ASIC's are also to the point of never getting your ROI. I don't want to discourage any of you not to mine.

Mining is critical to the Đogecoin network and any coins network. Continued mining by us is so important for many reasons. Network security can be compromised by the dreaded "51% attack." A 51% attack is when a person or group holds 51% or more of the hashing power of a coin. If they choose to, they can create a hard fork and start a new blockchain of their own. This would ruin the coin. Mining is also critical for continued transactions going forward on the network.

OK Shibes, thanks for hanging in there with me. Now, let's talk Đogecoin mining. How can you get your hands on some Đogecoins? You could buy some, but this is still a hassle. There are only a few places to buy Đoge without jumping through hoops or selling your soul to the Devil. You could beg for coins, but this is not very Shibe-like. Getting coins through tipping is good, but nothing beats getting coins through good old fashioned mining.

So, how can you mine? First, don't use your laptop. Many a Shibe has toasted a perfectly good laptop trying to use it for mining. Mining Scrypt coins with any graphics card will get that GPU toasty hot. Laptops don't cool very well.

The next thing we can use to mine is a Graphics Card (GPU). There are plenty of mining tutorials on /r/dogecoin, so we won't repeat them here. I think our time is best spent looking at the present options for equipment with which to mine. For those of you with GPU rigs, consider small ASIC's at this point. GPU's are at the stage where they are not cost effective anymore. I have made a spreadsheet to give you all a better picture of what's going on with equipment. (See Figure 1 below.)

As you can see from Figure 1, some ASIC miners look to be a profitable investment. They aren't. All of these miners will not return your investment after the next halvening in July. These figures also don't take into account difficulty increases or the rise/fall of the price of Ðogecoin in the future. The problem with these miners is they use too much electricity and their hashrates aren't high enough to make them profitable. What should you do? Well, you want to mine, and we have to secure the network. I suggest you do what I've done. I sold all my video cards on Ebay. I first bought the 5 chip Gridseed miners, then added Gridseed Blade miners as I could afford them. Fortunately, the prices of both have gone way down. I am holding off for more powerful ASIC miners coming in a few months. KNC, Fibbonacci, FlowerTech, MAT, Alcheminer and Bliss are all coming out with insane products. They will still be profitable if they make it to the market by September. Will they make it to the market in time? Are some of them scams? All good questions. I will keep you posted in every issue of VMW. Stay tuned in future articles for info on equipment, halvenings, merged mining, network security and mining other coins to get Ðogecoins. Put your hardhat on and get your pickaxe and start digging away.......

Tip Free1000:
D7heCcEttopHGTCtaECB43qN7zSUpQ5bvd

"YOU WANT TO MINE. AND WE NEED TO SECURE THE DOGECOIN NETWORK."

Figure 1. Mining Rig ROI

Product	USD Cost	Watts	Hash Rate	.11 KWH/day	Ð per day	ROI (Days)
Nvidia 750TI GPU	$179	65	300 Kh/s	$0.17	990	965
AMD R9 290X GPU	$399	275	900 Kh/s	$0.73	3000	1156
Gridseed 5Chip ASIC	$75	6	370 Kh/s	$0.02	1200	176
Gridseed Blade ASIC	$608	100	5200 Kh/s	$0.26	17000	102
Zeus Blizzard	$199	40	1260 Kh/s	$0.11	4000	142
Zeus Cyclone	$2,999	800	22000 Kh/s	$2.11	72000	124
GAWMiner Fury	$126	45	1300 Kh/s	$0.12	4200	88
GAWMiner Black Widow	$1,200	520	13500 Kh/s	$1.37	44000	81
GAWMiner Falcon	$2,250	1040	27000 Kh/s	$2.75	89000	76
GAWMiner War Machine	$4,450	2000	54000 Kh/s	$5.28	178000	75
Hashra Lunar Launcher	$1,250	485	14000 Kh/s	$1.28	46000	81
Hashra Lunar Lander	$2,275	820	26000 Kh/s	$2.16	86000	79
Hashra Lunar Lander 2	$4,500	1640	52000 Kh/s	$4.33	178000	78
Hashra Lunar Lander 3	$6,700	2460	78000 Kh/s	$6.49	258000	77
Innosilicon A2 2 module	$3,700	300	25000 Kh/s	$0.79	82000	127
Innosilicon A2 4 module	$10,900	600	50000 Kh/s	$1.58	165000	188
Innosilicon A2 5 module	$9,000	750	64000 Kh/s	$1.28	211000	121
Innosilicon A2 6 module	$10,200	900	77000 Kh/s	$2.38	255000	114

DR.LOWDOG

DOGES IN SPACE

Russian Space Doge : Laika (Лайка, "Barker")

Belka and Strelka

Some "Sirius" Facts:

Sirius is the brightest star in the night sky. With a visual apparent magnitude of −1.46, it is almost twice as bright as Canopus, the next brightest star.

Distance to Earth: 8.611 light years
Mass: 4.018E30 kg (2.02 Solar mass)
Radius: 1,190,000 km (1.711 R)
Surface temperature: 9,940 K
Magnitude: -1.46
Constellation: Canis Major

There are dogs in space suits, dogs on rockets, dogs communing with extraterrestrials, and we are sending Doge to the moon. What are these images bubbling out of our collective psyches? Why are we projecting dogs into space? We need to take space dogs seriously. They run deep in the human imagination and are poking their heads out now through Dogecoin. Space dogs have a history in both the culture of ancient astrology and modern space program.

Long before Scooby and Scrappy Doo, star gazers drew two dogs in the sky, one big and one small. The asterisms Canis Major and Canis Minor, the greater dog and lesser dog, are included in Ptolemy's 48 constellations. He compiled the set using ancient Greek, Egyptian and Babylonian sources from the libraries of Alexandria in the second century AD. They are the dogs of Orion and appear to the left of the hunter on opposite sides of the Milky Way.

Canis Major runs at the heels of Orion chasing the rabbit Lepus. The dog's head points toward Orion. At the tip of the nose shines the brightest star in the sky. This is the Dog Star, Sirius. The name, which first appeared in Hesiod, is derived from *seirios*, meaning intensely vibrating, sparkling or scorching. Think "Doge Intensifies." That's Sirius.

The rising of the sun beneath Sirius during the summer solstice coincided with the flooding of the Nile so Egyptians revered the star. Its hieroglyph, a dog, often appears on the monuments and temple walls throughout the Nile country. The term "dog days of summer" comes from this relationship between Sirius and hot summer sun.

The mythological association of the star Sirius with the dog is a cross-cultural phenomena. Chinese astronomers knew Sirius as *Tianlang*, 'celestial wolf,' or simply *Lang*, 'wolf'; it was said to symbolize invasion and plunder. In India, Sirius has been referred to as *Svana*, the dog of Prince Yudhistira.

In actuality, Sirius is a binary star system consisting of the brighter Sirius A orbited by the dimmer white dwarf Sirius B. The period of this cycle is approximately 50 years and gives the Sirius A system a helical path. The Dogon people of central Mali revere the star and have knowledge of its helical path. The ancient Egyptians had this same knowledge. The Dogon, seriously?

Orion has another dog, Canis Minor, the lesser dog. The smaller dog runs on the other side of the Milky Way as the greater dog. The little dog is a little less serious. Rather than chase rabbits this dog rides on top of a unicorn, Monoceros. Now that's silly. The medieval Arabic astronomers maintained the depiction of Canis Minor (*al-Kalb al-Asghar* in Arabic) as a dog. The constellation is made of two primary stars, Procyon in the belly of the little dog and Gomeisa at the head. The Arab names of these two stars translate to "Syrian Sirius" and "bleary eyed Sirius" respectively.

So what have we learned thus far?

- space dogs are serious and silly
- space dogs come in pair
- space dogs are intense and move around a lot
- humans like space dogs

Now we turn our gaze from ancient astrology to the modern space program. In the fifties and

The Doge Stars: Canis Major (left) and Canis Minor (right)

sixties the Soviet Union undertook a project of launching dogs into space to test the feasibility of human space flight. In total, the USSR sent a total of 57 dogs into both orbital and sub-orbital space flight. It was this scientific project that generates much of the visual iconography of the modern space dog and another manifestation of humans projecting dogs into space.

Perhaps the most famous Soviet space dog was Laika (Лайка, "Barker") who was the first animal to orbit the earth. Laika orbited the earth aboard Sputnik 2 on November 3, 1957. While this was a solo mission, most dogs were sent up into space in pairs.

Doge Pairs in Space:

- **Dezik (Дезик) and Tsygan (Цыган, "Gypsy") 1951,** 110 km altitude and safe landing
- **Lisa (Лиса, "Fox") and Ryzhik (Рыжик, "Ginger") 1954,** 100 km altitude and safe landing
- **Smelaya (Смелая, "Courageous") and Malyshka (Малышка, "Babe")1954,** such flight
- **Albina (Альбина) and Tsyganka (Цыганка, "Gypsy girl")** 1960, survived failed launch
- **Damka (Дамка, "Queen of checkers") and Krasavka (Красавка, "Little Beauty")** 1960, survived failed launch
- **Bars (Барс, "Snow leopard") and Lisichka (Лисичка, "Little Fox")** 1960, tragic launch
- **Pchyolka (Пчёлка, "Little Bee") and Mushka (Мушка, "Little Fly")** 1960, 1 day orbit, tragic re-entry
- **Veterok (Ветерок, "Light Breeze") and Ugolyok (Уголёк, "Coal")** 1966, 22 day orbit and safe landing

On two occasions the Soviets sent a pair a dogs into space accompanied by a rabbit. Canine cosmonauts Otvazhnaya (Отважная, "Brave One") and Snezhinka (Снежинка, "Snowflake") made a flight on July 2nd 1959 along with a rabbit named Marfusha (Марфуша, "Little Martha").

On August 19 1960 space dogs Belka (Белка, "Squirrel"), Strelka (Стрелка, "Arrow") and an unnamed rabbit spent a day in space aboard Korabl-Sputnik-2 (Sputnik 5) before safely returning to Earth.

What else did we learn?

- humans love space dogs
- space dogs are heros
- space dogs come in pairs
- space dogs like rabbits

But seriously, what does this mean for Dogecoin? Taking Doge to the moon is both a mythological and technological project. It is scientific poetry. While dog is fundamentally a terrestrial creature they have loftier aspirations. They look skyward as we. Dog will not only join us in our space missions, they will lead the way. Dogecoin is going to the moon on an epic scale.

Tip Dr. Low Dog:
DRLowUsgPGKRfKZorx3mUx56kNT2ZDNtcs

DISCOVER THE

Moon

a very beautiful vacation spot

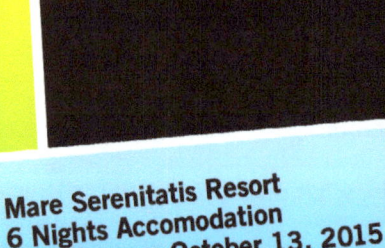

**Mare Serenitatis Resort
6 Nights Accomodation
Departure on October 13, 2015**

Starting From

1 DOGE

Per Person

Moon Holiday Package

- First class accomodations on our Dogecoin rocketship
- VIP seating at the Lunar Iditarod miniature rover race
- A tour of Vallis Alpes at sunrise
- Black tie dinner at the top of the Mons Ampère Space Needle
- Regolith skiing down Montes Archimedes
- Tickets to the Dorsa Dana Disco
- Experience the finest in freeze-dried cuisine

**BOOK NOW!
www.verymuchwow.com**

ALBUQUERQUE, NEW MEXICO
info@verymuchwow.com

Taking off from Spaceport America!

DOGECOIN, WOW

How can I explain Dogecoin to someone new? I can't, kind of. It's really a magical place on the internet I happened to stumble upon after reading comments in a reddit post. It was a little over-whelming at first, and soon I found myself googling everything I could about Dogecoin. I subbed to /r/dogecoin the very first time I found it, and after learning a bit more I figured sticking around could be fun. The transformation into becoming a shibe was a long one, and I fought a lot in the beginning. I finally caved in when the fundraiser for buying the shirts was circulating, it was at the second post I saw about the fundraiser that I decided just to jump in.

Looking at all the things that Dogecoin has done, it surprised me quite a bit how much this new community was able to do. After I bought the shirt, I started to become a little more invested into the subreddit over the next few days. I started saving links related to doge, economics, news sites, merchant sites that accept doge, saving comments so I could help the new shibes. It was around this point that I had accepted by fate and embraced being a shibe. For better or worse, I had finally started to buy dogecoin with whatever I could spare. I began to visit reddit and go right to /r/dogecoin to see what was new, and participating in conversations about doge.

At this point, I had saved quite a few guides and links that I could use later for educating new shibes. Tipping, it's intoxicating. Tipping and being tipped gave me this good feeling and soon I had started buying $10 of doge instead of $5. If you ever want to get a rush of being appreciated for even one afternoon, then doing a giveaway can help you achieve this. I may have realized at this point I was a kinda-shibe, but when I did my first giveaway and made it timed the first thing I did when it hit front page was to post helpful links for new shibes. It was while looking at the post after I had edited the new links in the sense of being a true shibe washed over me.

Buying dogecoin to buy items in dogecoin was the obvious next step. To date I have bought three things in doge: a key chain, a bronze coin, and a doge sticker. I currently have converted $100 over the past few weeks into 222,690 dogecoins. If the market price goes down that just means that I get more Dogecoin for my buck, which I don't mind at all.

So far the roller coaster that is /r/dogecoin has been exciting, funny, sad, and all of the above. At its heart, the community is quite pure and honest, genuinely wanting to help Dogecoin grow and fund new and exciting fundraisers whatever they may be. I can say for a fact that even if Dogecoin doesn't last forever, the way has been paved for new ideas and movements to sweep across the internet and potentially change lives. There is also one more thing I am certain of that explains my feelings toward the Dogecoin community.

I regret nothing, and I would do it all again even if Dogecoin crashes. To the moon fellow shibes, to the moon we will go.

Tip MiniPapaTank:
D7e3JmukFt5Bg9xrRoxgxQcnHHWNaL9wUU

CORE DEVELOPEMENT ROUNDUP
JUNE 2014 | NEW 1.7 CLIENT RELEASE | LOOKING AHEAD TO 1.8

Welcome to the June Dogecoin Core development roundup! This regular column will be a summary of the main themes and announcements about Dogecoin Core ("Dogecoin Core" is the reference client, as opposed to light clients such as Multidoge). This month's article summarizes the recent 1.7 Client release and the consequent steps we are able to take towards 1.8.

The main drivers for recent Dogecoin Core development have been a need to improve performance, and the building of a rock-solid base for those adopting Dogecoin.These stem from issues with the earlier 1.5 and 1.6 clients, which had performance problems when used for mining and other high-end applications.

For the recently released 1.7 client, the software has effectively been completely rebuilt using the Bitcoin Core 0.9 client as its base. This update brings significant speed and stability improvements to the client, as well as usability improvements such as coin control (which lets you choose inputs to a transaction) and a redesigned interface for receiving payments.

By rebuilding the client based on Bitcoin, as opposed to Litecoin, we have also simplified the process of adopting later improvements from the Bitcoin Core client.

1.7 is a significant improvement over 1.6. It is a recommended update but not a mandatory one. As always, it is crucial that you back up your wallet file ("wallet.dat") before updating the software. You can do this from within the existing 1.6 client by navigating to the "File" menu and selecting "Backup wallet." Alternatively the file can be found at "%AppData%\Roaming\DogeCoin" on Windows if you wish to do it manually, or need to restore the file. Please also note that once upgraded from 1.6 to 1.7, the wallet file cannot (reliably) be opened in 1.6.

With the OpenSSL "Heartbleed" security issue barely out of the news, many have asked whether the Dogecoin client is vulnerable. Dogecoin Core currently uses SSL only for RPC over SSL. For most people that won't mean anything, and it's an extremely unusual setup. RPC is the protocol for sending commands to a Dogecoin client from another piece of software. RPC over SSL would only be used if you are sending commands to the client over a network. This is generally discouraged as it risks security holes such as Heartbleed (or whatever bug is found next). The 1.7 client is based on a fixed version, so anyone using RPC over SSL should upgrade immediately.

The next update to Dogecoin Core is shaping up nicely. Version 1.7.2 brings in a number of bug fixes and tweaks (at the last count just under 150) from the Bitcoin Core 0.9.2 client. I am also personally working on "payment protocol" support, with the hope it will be ready for 1.7.2. Payment protocol, originally defined in Bitcoin Improvement Proposal (BIP) 0070-0072, is a way of streamlining requests for payments, sending payments to a merchant, and confirmation that those payments have been received.

The typical process for payment protocol is that the merchant produces a payment request which is sent to the user's Dogecoin client. The user's client requests confirmation that the payment should be sent, and if authorised by the user creates a transaction, signs it, and sends it back to the merchant, along with details of where a refund should be sent if needed. Finally, the merchant relays the transaction to the network, and sends confirmation of receipt of payment back to the wallet. This has a number of advantages:

1. The amount and payment address is passed to the wallet programmatically, removing the risk of a cut & paste or typo error.

ROSS NICOLL

2. Payment requests can be cryptographically signed, enabling receiver confidence in the sender of the request. This is useful in scenarios such as payment requests being sent over unencrypted links, where a man-in-the-middle attack could facilitate a substitution of the genuine request with a fake request leading to a modified payment address.

3. Because the transaction is sent directly to the merchant, there is essentially no delay for the merchant in seeing the transaction on the network.

4. A refund address can be provided to the merchant, simplifying the process of refunding a payment if needed (for example order cancellation).

The original payment protocol was designed with Bitcoin in mind, and does not readily support other coins. For Dogecoin we are modifying the protocol to keep compatibility with the majority of cryptocurrencies, as well as to ensure that payment requests for Bitcoin and Dogecoin cannot be mixed up. We are producing a sample merchant application in order to fully test these changes. Further details of both the changes and the merchant application will be released in due course.

Looking to the future, Dogecoin 0.8 is planned to follow Bitcoin 0.10's development, and is anticipated to include major improvements to the architecture of the code. This is a key prerequisite to making significant changes to the user interface of Dogecoin Core without causing problems when integrating new functionality from Bitcoin Core.

While following in another coin's footsteps in this way may not be terribly exciting, it is the most efficient use of our development resources. The stability of the current release and the in-depth testing of changes being added to the client reflect both our intent to provide the rock-solid base that one would expect from a major currency, and our desire to build confidence in the quality of the software.

Lastly, for our newer shibes who may be struggling with the first synchronisation of the block chain, please note that you can use a "bootstrap file" to significantly speed up the sync process. Download links and full details on how to use the bootstrap file are available from So Chain at https://bootstrap.chain.so/.

Ross Nicoll is one of the core Dogecoin developers.

Ross requests that instead of tipping him, you send donations to the

Central Dogecoin Development Fund

The Central Fevelopment Fund is a fund managed by Langerhans - our lead developer for the reference client. It pays developers who contribute to Dogecoin Core, both to reward them for their work, and to offset costs such as hosting, server space, etc.

Details of payments from the fund are posted to the /r/dogecoindev subreddit.

So Chain's link to the Dev Fund:
https://chain.so/address/devfund

Donate to the Core Development Fund:

D6AyeHunfkVcarXvw4S4gjNT1rokp5KRK6

The Dogemarket Review

Wow. It's been an eventful month to have come on board as *Very Much Wow*'s market analyst.

Dogecoin hit its lowest value against Bitcoin at the end of May, after a series of rapid falls beginning on May 19. From the number of particularly high volume trading days, it appears that a number of more cautious investors responded to the drop in price by exiting the Doge market, or substantially reducing their holdings.

However, June 2 saw a sudden overcorrection in the market, with the Doge trading at around 65 Satoshi on most exchanges, before stabilising around the 55 Satoshi mark towards the end of the week.

DOGE/BTC Exchange Rate: Last 30 days to Jun 13, 2014

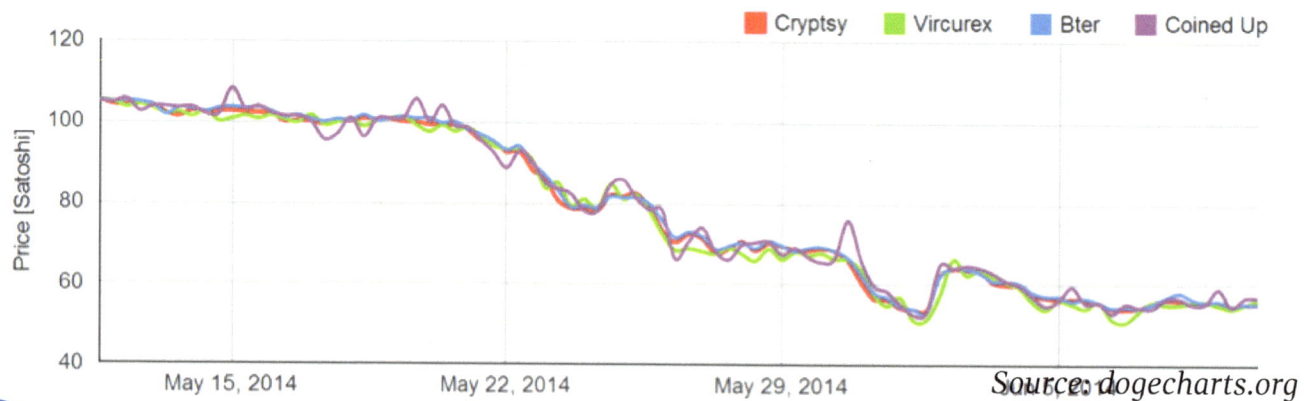

Source: dogecharts.org

The recent price volatility has left some holders hoping for more stable markets in coming months, in spite of investor concern over April's price stagnation. Fluctuations in trading volume have also levelled out this week, a trend that may help to firm up exchange rates if it continues.

The market depth as at June 13 also shows a lot of support around the 50 to 54 Satoshi level, with investors keen to enter the market just below the current price point. This may provide a much needed buffer against further rapid price drops in the short term.

Market Depth: June 13, 2014 04:00 GMT

buy orders

price	Σ [DOGE]	Σ [BTC]	Cryptsy	Vircurex	Bter	Coined Up
56	1,382,974	0.774466				0.774466
55	4,951,620	2.723391	2.080328		0.507043	0.136021
54	56,318,673	30.412083	27.945100	0.052543	2.414441	
53	30,550,303	16.191660	15.134354	0.128340	0.927377	0.001590
52	23,677,332	12.312213	7.026038	0.067548	5.212386	0.006240
51	12,565,011	6.408156	5.685567	0.266603	0.061200	0.394786
50	27,689,001	13.844500	10.003058	0.094020	1.473150	2.274272
49	8,467,498	4.149074	3.129426		1.019550	0.000098
48	8,212,409	3.941956	3.941383			0.000574
47	4,770,353	2.242066	2.199676			0.042389
46	2,076,191	0.955048	0.954963			0.000085
45	7,935,769	3.571096	3.245365		0.166800	0.158931
44	9,495,025	4.177811	4.176595		0.001139	0.000077
43	3,216,568	1.383124	1.246151		0.132600	0.004373
42	910,080	0.382234	0.343264	0.033600	0.005300	0.000069
41	1,985,438	0.814029	0.809864		0.004100	0.000066
40	3,831,580	1.532632	0.908420		0.140150	0.484062
39	27,654,626	10.785304	0.715725		10.002700	0.066880
38	3,909,924	1.485771	1.094684		0.012691	0.378396
37	6,779,332	2.508353	0.658301		1.110000	0.740052

sell orders

price	Σ [DOGE]	Σ [BTC]	Cryptsy	Vircurex	Bter	Coined Up
56	26,787,448	15.000971	13.057391		1.943244	0.000335
57	47,280,878	26.950101	22.597613	0.142221	4.208229	0.002037
58	10,580,578	6.136735	5.464509	0.022451	0.649776	
59	15,203,129	8.969846	8.772550	0.070120	0.127175	
60	25,847,104	15.508262	14.208015	0.531863	0.765867	0.002517
61	10,302,359	6.284439	5.742959	0.006100	0.535380	
62	9,691,473	6.008713	5.277635	0.107804	0.623275	
63	21,410,004	13.488303	11.647501	0.448968	1.391835	
64	10,262,731	6.568148	5.204624	0.063872	1.299651	
65	14,642,635	9.517713	6.589915	0.013236	1.098730	1.815832
66	28,095,416	18.542974	17.029943	0.051965	1.447867	0.013200
67	1,830,623	1.226518	1.212504	0.009024	0.004990	
68	2,414,873	1.642114	1.220863	0.068559	0.352692	
69	16,902,051	11.662415	10.929746	0.116650	0.616019	
70	14,002,067	9.801447	8.791781	0.587055	0.422341	0.000269
71	13,235,422	9.397149	9.306271		0.090879	
72	12,448,641	8.963021	8.938197	0.000144	0.024681	
73	17,978,280	13.124144	13.034384	0.042595	0.047165	
74	5,737,726	4.245917	4.020008		0.225909	
75	17,805,608	13.354206	13.186547	0.121834	0.045825	

Source: dogecharts.org

Although the recent price falls have left investors disappointed, the more general downward trend in prices from February's dramatic highs doesn't come as a complete surprise. Early enthusiasm and ramping of the currency – however well intended – was certainly a factor in boosting the price earlier in the year. If it is to flourish in the long term, the Doge will need to see more sustainable growth, and some moderation in the market's sensitivity to investor expectations.

Market Capitalisation

The week's price recovery is reflected in Dogecoin's market capitalisation, placing it firmly within coinmarketcap.com's top ten currencies. The Doge's market cap is currently sitting alongside that of Ripple's math-based bridge currency, XRP. Both are sitting at a cap of around US$32m as at Jun 13, well above Namecoin at US$17m, and trailing Peercoin at US$37.5m.

Tip Helen:
DBHcWoFVjQfRncvsD12yvvdaz6GgWTEPKA

Very Language!
The SuchIndex of Shibe-centric Thought
By "Very Much Doctor" Bob
Vice President for Shibemetrics
Such Institute of Wow

What is Dogecoin? What does Dogecoin *mean*? One way to study these questions is to investigate the way people talk and write about Dogecoin.

This month we present some results from a study of the content of *Very Much Wow* (**VMW**), which is a rich source of contemporary Shibe-istic thought. For this study, the basic approach was to identify and track significant words in the text of VMW #1 and #2, (May and June, 2014). This technique may reveal underlying meanings and trends over time.

We focus here on the frequency of three terms: "Such," "Much," and "Wow." *Figure 1* shows the frequencies of these terms in the **May** versus the **June** issue of **Very Much Wow**, along with the frequencies in a comparison document, the Gettysburg Address (A. Lincoln, 1863).

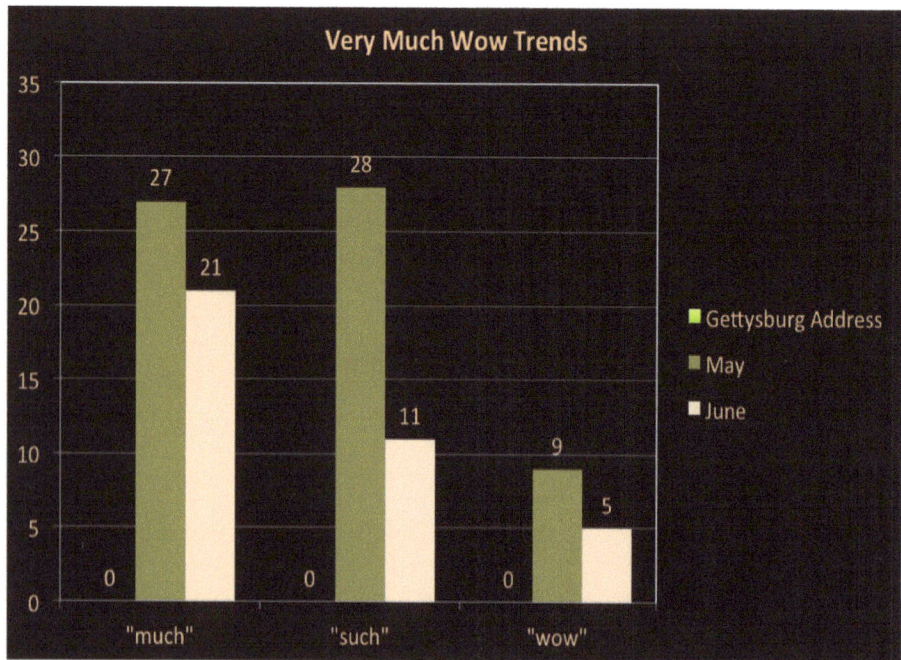

Figure 1. Very Trend: Three Key Words from *Very Much Wow*. The *Gettysburg Address* is included for comparison.

Shibeham Lincoln

To summarize these numbers, we propose the following Shibemetric formula, the **SuchMuchWow Index** (*SuchIndex*):

Definition 1:
$$SuchIndex := \frac{freq(\text{such}) - freq(\text{much})}{freq(\text{wow})}$$

Intuitively, the *SuchIndex* expresses the relative *suchness* versus *muchness*, balanced for the level of *wowness*. Some scholars theorize that this index correlates to the strength of Shibe-centric verbalizations.

Table 1 gives the *SuchIndex* for the data in Figure 1. In this case, we see a distinct increase and a change of sign in the *SuchIndex* from May to June. Additional data is necessary to evaluate this possible trend.

Table 1. SuchIndex for *Very Much Wow* May and June, and the *Gettysburg Address*

Source	SMWindex
Gettysburg Address	*Can't compute*
Very Much Wow - May	-0.11
Very Much Wow - June	2.0

Abraham Lincoln: Secret Shibe?

While many believe that Abraham Lincoln might have been an early proponent of Dogecoin[1], these data seem to show that either he did not use Dogecoin, or chose to conceal his support from the public. This current study does not resolve this question.

Summary

Wow! Much Knowledge! Amaze Science! Of the Shibes, for the Shibes, and by the Shibes!

Methodology

The data was assembled by extracting all the text from the PDF files for *Very Much Wow* issues 1 and 2, using a proprietary algorithm. The name of the publication ("Very Much Wow") and related terms such as "verymuchwow.com" were excluded from the counts.

The *Shibemetrics* column from VMW #2 was excluded from the counts. Including our own text in our analysis seemed to be too difficult to interpret. Including or excluding the *Shibemetrics* article did not substantially change the overall results.

A similar analysis was conducted on the text of the Gettysburg Address.

Data Sources:
VeryMuchWow: http://verymuchwow.com
Gettysburg Address by Abraham Lincoln (1863):
http://en.wikipedia.org/wiki/Gettysburg_Address#Text_of_Gettysburg_Address

Tip "Very Much Doctor" Bob:
DRAhz9heD2SVmtZB5D2WgHwmvxudz7kLzk

1 For example, Dr. G. Garner suggests that President Lincoln may have patented a steam powered "dog mining apparatus," which would be the earliest documented cryptomining rig (see Grant Garner, "Lincoln's Unacknowledged Patents", Journal of Fund Extraction and Absorption, Dec. 31, 1969)).

PHOTO of the MONTH

DOGESHIRT | /U/FUCTARP ON REDDIT

Fuctarp has generously donated his winning
photo payment back to *Very Much Wow*! Thanks,
Fuctarp! He will be giving us an interview on the
ways in which shibes help each other through
depression in our next issue of *Very Much Wow*!
WHAT A SHIBE!

ART of the MONTH

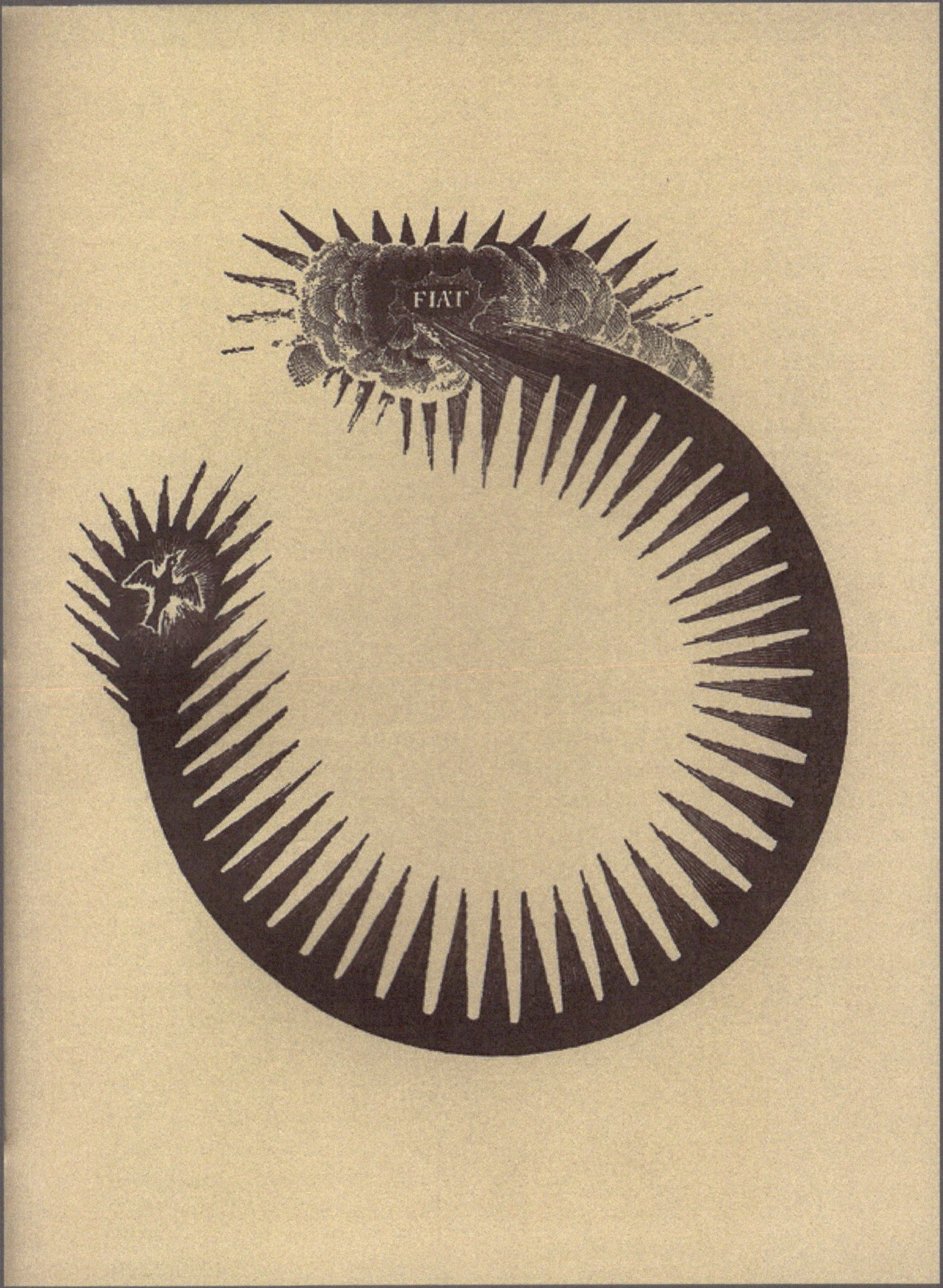

ORIGINAL ART BY /U/PLUTOWASAPLANET

DD8cSCpP7P7Y6iJpjuhmKZjhLLGF4zytJq

WOW MUCH TALK

ROBERT MCGRATH

You Shall Not Crucify The Internet On This Cross of Bitcoin

In recent months there has been an explosion of interest in cryptocurrencies, led by the Ur-currency, Bitcoin[1], but notably also featuring a plethora of "alt-coins"- alternative cryptocurrencies. Contemporary cryptocurrencies are technically similar, and easily interchangeable with each other and with conventional currencies, goods, and services. This situation raises significant questions, such as:

Why are there so many more or less interchangeable cryptocurrencies? If they are technically similar, how are they different?

As we examine these questions, today's cryptocurrencies have given us a "teachable moment," which leads us to relearn the significance of "money," and to discover lessons from history. These lessons are surprisingly deep, and surprisingly divorced from the information technology that underpins current developments.

WHY IS BITCOIN "EXPENSIVE," AND WHY SHOULD IT MATTER?

For at least the last seventy years, conventional currency has been issued by central banks, with the amount in circulation set by policy. These currencies are valuable because they are legal tender and fiercely protected by the government: i.e., by legal 'fiat.' There is no fixed limit to the amount of money that can be in circulation, and the amount tends to increase over time - if nothing else, following the level of economic activity, but often to stimulate economic activity.

In contrast, cryptocurrencies are designed to operate more like pre-modern asset-backed currencies, e.g., coins and bullion. For example, the Ur-coin, Bitcoin, is designed to operate as virtual

"gold." The amount of Bitcoin in the world is limited by how much has been successfully "mined," and is ultimately limited to a finite number of coins (21 million total).[2]

These technical parameters of Bitcoin are set by software,[3] which make it increasingly difficult to mine coins (i.e., the math problem is computationally difficult). The result is that there are relatively few Bitcoins (especially compared to, say, dollars or yen), and the number is growing slowly, and will eventually reach a stable maximum.

These features mean that Bitcoins are rare, and will stay rare. No matter how many people use them, or how much the economy grows, the number and growth of Bitcoins will not increase. Enthusiasts claim this means they will be "a stable store of value" (which is also claimed for gold), though this has not been observed empirically yet (for either metallic gold or Bitcoin).

It is critical to realize that the parameters of a cryptocurrency protocol can be set to different values; effectively creating alternative cryptocurrencies. In fact, there are dozens, if not hundreds of such cryptocurrencies (also know as 'alt-coins') extant, with parameters set to different numbers.

Many alt-coins have set the technical parameters to allow faster mining (via an easier math problem with more generous payouts), with higher or expanding limits on the total coins. Generally speaking, this means that there can be more coins in play compared to Bitcoin, with rapid increases, and possibly a higher ceiling on the number of coins in circulation.

The result is that more people can get and use such alt-coins, while each individual coin is typically worth "less," as measured against Bitcoin,

1 https://bitcoin.org/en/

2 Nakamoto, Satoshi, Bitcoin: A Peer-to-Peer Electronic Cash System. 2009. http://bitcoin.org/bitcoin.pdf
3 Apparently, the 'fiat' of unelected programmers is philosophically different from the 'fiat' of unelected bankers and politicians.

other currencies (such as dollars), or in purchasing power. Basically, these alt-coins are "cheaper" (or "weaker") currencies than Bitcoin.

So what difference does it make? You can always trade between cryptocurrencies, to convert, say, to or from Bitcoin, and you can always trade into conventional currencies, such as dollars. Why would we want more than one cryptocurrency? If we have more than one, what would be the "best" setting(s) for the parameters?

Let's look at history for some insight.

A Lesson From U.S. History

The history of the United States has featured numerous controversies surrounding experiments with currencies.[4] The second half of the nineteenth century saw a particularly important episode, the adoption of the gold-backed dollar. This adventure in monetary policy gives us a precedent and grounds for understanding possible economic and social effects of multiple asset-like currencies.

During the 1860-65 Civil War, the US was forced to print paper money to finance the war effort. The federal dollars ("greenbacks") were backed by faith in the government, with only a vague promise to redeem them for gold. During the same period, the economy saw significant inflation, with prices in the North doubling in five years. The losing southern states experienced general devastation and massive inflation of their own paper currency, and were then subsumed into the federal system at the end of the war.

At the end of hostilities, the US government sought to "stabilize" the currency and prices by returning to gold-backed currency. This policy brought the US in line with European trading partners and intentionally deflated prices until they were nearly equivalent to levels in 1860. At the same time as the gold backing for the currency was being "resumed" (i.e., greenbacks were replaced by gold certificates), silver coinage was also ended. At that point, the US was on the gold standard, with all currency backed by gold reserves.[5]

4 If Eskimos are said to have 100 words for "snow," Americans must surely have 1,000,000 words for "money."
5 See perhaps, Eichengreen, Barry, *As Good as Gold - By What Standard?*, in *Second Thoughts: Myths and Morals of U.S. Economic History*, D.N. McCloskey, Editor. Oxford University Presss, New York, 1993,

The gold standard did not actually provide much stability, as the amount of gold fluctuates, and, in any case, gold does not prevent bank runs and other panics. The policy did cause significant deflation: in the first years of the gold standard, the dollar value of many goods and services fell by 25% or more. Such deflation may be good for holders of gold, but it is bad for anyone selling commodities such as grain or labor. And it was very bad indeed for borrowers, because loans and mortgages were denominated in fixed dollars, which means the amount owed effectively increased over time.

The overall effect was serious contraction and hardship, especially in agriculture. Farmers complained of paying for inputs with borrowed dollars, getting paid less and less for outputs, and having to repay debts in even more valuable dollars.

One upshot of the hard times was a political uprising which advocated a variety of policies including monetary reforms intended to reverse the deflation attributed to the gold standard. The "greenback" party advocated a return to fiat currency, while the "free silver" movement advocated unlimited silver coinage. Both of these policies were aimed to end the peg of the dollar to gold, increase the amount of money in circulation, inflate commodity prices, and generally stimulate the economy.

Out of the period arose the People's (Populist) Party, which adopted a combination of these positions, and elected quite a few representatives and Senators. The high water mark of the Populist Party was the presidential runs of William Jennings Bryan in 1896 and again in 1900. His famous 1896 convention speech blasted the gold standard and the economic interests that it served, and famously proclaimed,

"You shall not press down upon the brow of labor this crown of thorns; you shall not crucify mankind on this cross of gold."[6]

His campaign was unsuccessful, but laid the foundation for many reforms of the early twentieth century.

79-87
6 Bryan, William Jenning, *The 'Cross of Gold' Speech*, in *An American Primer*, D.J. Bourstein, Editor. Meridian, New York, 1985, 539-604

YOU SHALL NOT CRUCIFY THE INTERNET ON THIS CROSS OF BITCOIN?

It is critical to understand that the *gold standard* versus *free silver* conflict became part of the larger political narrative of nineteenth century America. Eastern political elites - masters of industrial capitalism - dreamed of America as an outward looking global power - one with a gold standard. Western and Southern farmers and workers, in an inward looking agrarian country - wanted a land with plentiful silver coinage and paper money.[7]

These competing narratives (and related themes about science, religion, race, and so on) had meaning and power of their own. Monetary policy was incorporated into these narratives and thereby given meaning far beyond the merits of coinage and amount of money in circulation.

Just as neither sliver nor gold is intrinsically "more valuable," alternative cryptocurrencies are technically interchangeable. But the narratives and communities committed to one or the other are quite distinct, far more so than any technical difference might account for. The lines of battle are not the same as 1896 (though they are surprisingly similar in some cases[8]), but they are very familiar from the overall political economy.

THE STORIES WE TELL (AND LIVE OUT)

To draw out nineteenth century parallels, we can see powerful, wealthy interests that support Bitcoin (Silicon Valley, Wall Street), making much the same claims about Bitcoin as used to be made about gold: stories about "honest money," "confidence," "stability," and "universality." The Bitcoin community also tells a narrative about "bold Internet entrepreneurs," "disrupting" and revolutionizing money and everything else. Some enthusiasts emphasize the disruption of economic power, envisioning displacing the wealthy institutions of Wall Street. Others imagine seceding from the political structure altogether, to create a virtual, "peer to peer," "off shore" economy that "cannot be regulated or taxed."

Altcoins tell a variety of other narratives. Some are simply less expensive versions of Bitcoin, perhaps an opportunity to make a killing. Advocates for these cryptocurrencies seem to enact Oedipal stories of sibling and parental rivalry with the patriarch, Bitcoin, and other sibling alt-coins, making forceful claims to be "just as good" as rival coins.

Other cryptocurrencies have been incorporated into deep and old stories about identity, culture, and values. We see, for example, "national" cryptocurrencies, such as Spain (SpainCoin[9]), Israel (Isracoin[10]), and Iceland (AuroraCoin[11]). Separatist movements, too, have dreamed of cryptocurrencies for their putative future state, such as (maybe-soon-devolved) Scotland or an (imagined) independent Republic of Venice. And one group has floated an "official" cryptocurrency for the "Traditional Lakota Nation" (MazaCoin[12]). These cryptocurrencies have become part of long standing stories of cultural identity and sovereignty.

The narrative need not be ancient, it just needs to be an appealing story. Some cryptocurrencies address specific goals, such as supporting education (Educoin[13]) or crowdsourcing science (Gridcoin[14]). These currencies carry "value" to their community of users, though not necessarily trying to be a general-purpose currency. The uniquely conceived Confessioncoin[15] seems to manufacture value out of thin air by providing a digital mechanism for personal atonement.

---

7 See perhaps, Dighe, Ranjit S., ed. *The Historian's Wizard of Oz: Reading L. Frank Baum's Classic as a Political and Monetary Allegory.* Praeger: Westport, 2002.

8 Elsewhere in his famous "Cross of Gold" speech, Bryan declares, "There are two ideas of government. There are those who believe that if you will only legislate to make the well-to-do prosperous their prosperity will leak through on those below. The Democratic idea, however, has been that if you legislate to make the masses prosperous their prosperity will find its way up through every class with rests upon them." More than one hundred years later, this is still a crystal clear statement about American politics in the last 35 years.

9 http://spaincoin.org/en/
10 http://www.isracoin.org/
11 http://auroracoin.org/
12 http://www.mazacoin.org/
13 http://educoin.cc/
14 https://www.gridcoin.us/
15 http://www.confessioncoin.com/

THE DOGECOIN NARRATIVE

In fact, a cryptocurrency narrative does not need to be "serious" to be successful. It only needs to attract an active community. The undoubted paradigm in this category is Dogecoin[16]. Dogecoin is a considered a "meme-based cryptocurrency,"[17] which invites its users to act out an absurdist play.

The Dogecoin narrative arose partly to be "not Bitcoin," and suggests that "value" is found through community, good humor, and gift giving. Where the Bitcoin story stars wealthy Venture Capitalists[18], Dogecoin has eschewed VC[19] and promulgated an enthusiastic "Fan"[20] culture. Dogecoin's community is invited to enact roles in a story, and to "succeed" by playing nicely together.[21]

Dogecoin is a particularly clear case of my thesis: the cryptocurrency itself is technically interchangeable with other cryptocurrencies, but it has a completely different narrative that has attracted different people, and different behavior.

CONCLUSION

The "cryptocurrency rush" of the early twenty first century is based on newly created technology, and sometimes is presented as a revolutionary and unprecedented development. In fact, the technology recreates many well known issues worked through in earlier years. Furthermore, the technical controversies are tiny and insignificant.

Cryptocurrencies themselves are technically simple to create, and present the creators with the opportunity to invent whatever uses and meanings they wish for their new digital "money". In this, they are an absolutely fascinating technology.

But I have argued that just as in earlier periods, concepts of digital "money" have been incorporated into much larger cultural narratives, into stories about identity, morality, and meaning. Cryptocurrencies, like other forms of money, play an important role, inviting us to play roles in the participatory theater surrounding them. In this sense, cryptocurrencies are not at all "transformative," they are actually just another front in multiple ongoing narratives about right and wrong, and who is in charge.

— — — — —

Robert E. McGrath is a retired software engineer and social scientist, currently interested in digitally augmented communities and IT that strengthens local communities. He blogs and writes about various topics, including augmented reality, personal fabrication, "the future of work", and cryptocurrency communities. He lives in Urbana, Illinois.

Blog: http://robertmcgrath.wordpress.com/

You may tip Robert at:
D83H9bB72twL6AyBnYfoN5W5KhG1qDvFb5

16 http://dogecoin.com/
17 This is a sophisticatedly ironic claim, since all money is both a meme and meme-based.
18 E.g., Marc Andreessen, http://youtu.be/iir5J6Z3Z1Q
19 http://www.dailydot.com/business/dogecoin-venture_capital-rejected-jackson_palmer/
20 Exhibit A: *Very Much Wow* magazine. http://verymuchwow.com
21 E.g., the Dogecoin party in February 2014, which featured costumes, dogs, and a march on Wall Street. http://youtu.be/gzljN5e_JG0

*Help! We're locked up in the Bernalillo County jail
and all we have to read are these %^$#! Very Much Wow magazines!!!!*

A VERY MUCH WOW PHOTO CONTEST!

Take a photograph of *Very Much Wow* in the Wild!
You may win one of several Dogecoin prizes!

First Place winner will be awarded 75K Dogecoins!

Post your photograph at /r/dogecoin or discuss.dogecoin.com
and send us a link to your entry!

Your entry will be judged on creativity, humor, your sense of
community, shibeliness, and artistic quality!

The winners will be determined by a discussion and vote
amongst the *Very Much Wow* Editorial and Writing Staff!

Send a link to your entry to: editor@verymuchwow.com

OVER 25K UNIQUE READERS

CATCH THE MOON

ADVERTISE
WITH VERY MUCH WOW!
PRINT AND ONLINE

3 and 6 MONTH DISCOUNT PACKAGES!
EMAIL: EDGAR@VERYMUCHWOW.COM
FOR FRIENDLY, PERSONALIZED SERVICE!

ASK ABOUT OUR NEW FREE COMMUNITY AD SPACE

A REVIEW OF DOGE SLEDDING

Most of the Doge related games on the market today are clones of other popular games with a minor Shibe theme overlayed. Doge Sledding, available on both Apple and Android devices, by XdebugX, provides a nice change of pace from this trend. Searching on both marketplaces revealed no other mobile games that are quite like it. Unfortunately, this does leave the game to stand on its own design merit, where it leaves a lot to be desired.

In Doge Sledding, players control a dog in a bobsleigh as it races down one of five unique tracks. Players can choose from four different dogs, including a Shiba Inu, and several different bobsleigh designs with which to race. Once a player chooses a dog, a bobsleigh, and a track, they can select between two different game modes, each of which offers both easy and hard levels of difficulty.

The first game mode is Coin Chase, where players are tasked with collecting Dogecoins as they progress down the track and attempt to avoid touching items that cause you to lose Dogecoins. The second mode is Timed Race, which is a straightforward challenge to complete the course as quickly as possible.

The game has a reasonably strong design for the 3D art assets. The dogs and bobsleighs are decently modeled and textured, and look overall satisfying. The track environments are easily the best feature of the game, as they look and feel unique and fun. Unfortunately, the art design falls extremely flat on the 2D elements and user interface. The menus feel too busy and cluttered while the heads up display and controls in-game are confusing.

The true downside to this game lies in the actual gameplay. The controls are almost impossible to use and feel unresponsive at best. The only control players have over their bobsleigh is the ability to control speed and to rotate oneself upside-down, which feel almost completely trivial.

I frequently found myself falling off the track randomly or having the game suddenly restart the track midway through a run without warning. The bobsleigh would also often end up sideways in the track, and since players cannot turn the bobsleigh on that axis, it would remain stuck like this until it bumped around enough to correct itself. Runs were sometimes not even completable due to consistent restarting problems, and I could not locate a pause menu that would allow me to quit back to the main menu, forcing me to kill the process for the game in the task manager of my device to restart the game.

Doge Sledding is a step in the right direction for Doge themed games in that it is an original game designed from the ground up with Doge in mind, instead of being a copy of another successful title. Despite this, I cannot recommend the game whosoever, as I found it to be nearly unplayable at several points. The game feels more like an early alpha test that someone threw finished 3D assets into, instead of a polished and tested game.

WOW

"The track environments are easily the best feature of the game, as they look and feel unique and fun."

DOGE SLEDDING

Tip Jyro:
D6SbM3coVCo7uYrqJZBMPJbSb476e5AhfM

JYRO BLADE

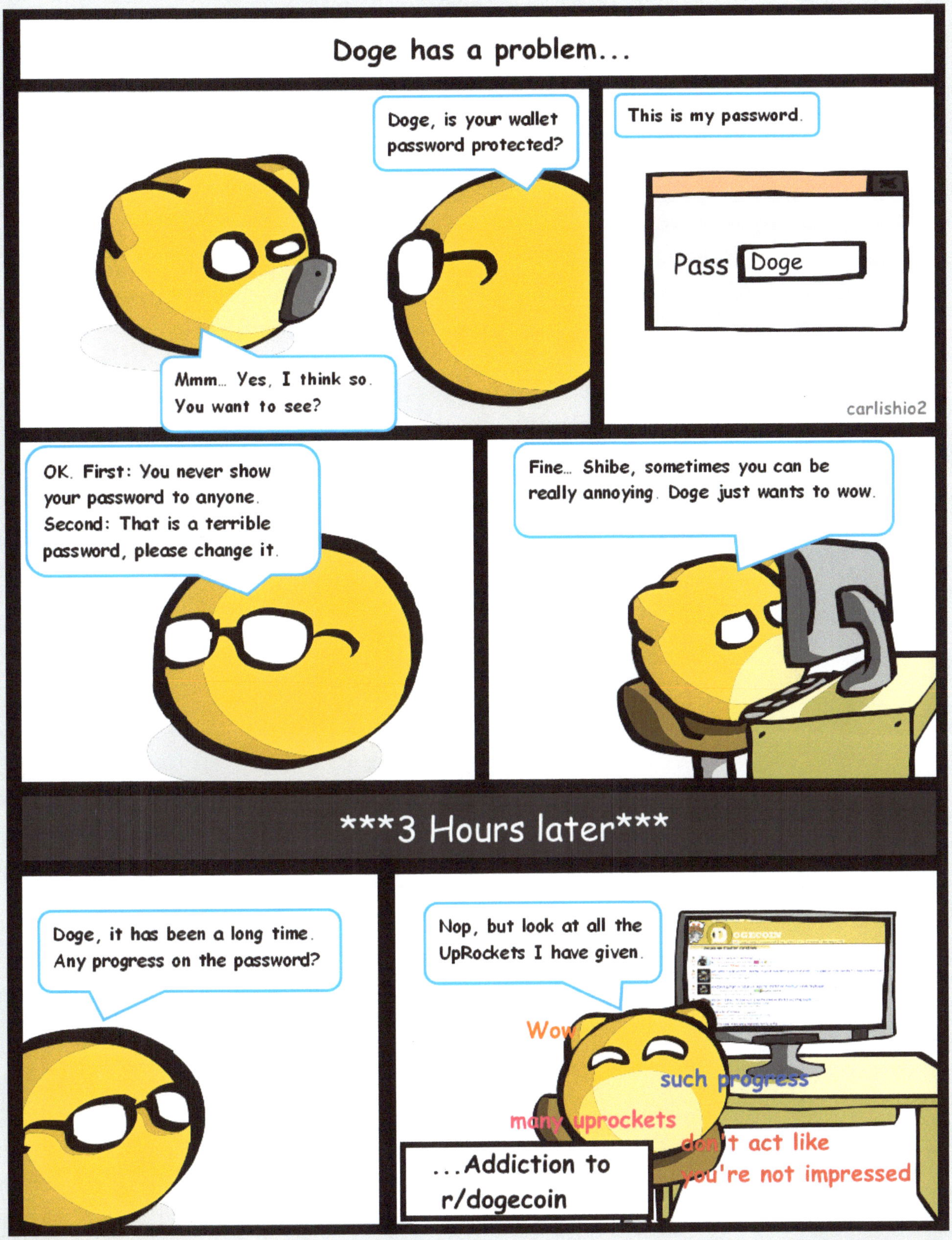

CLAY MICHAEL GILLESPIE

FAMED "GODZILLA" RECAPTURES THE CITY AND THE SCREEN

Smashing onto the big screen, Godzilla stars in another rebirth of this monster-sized franchise. There we go, now all the puns are out of my system. Debuting at $100 million domestically and $90 million overseas, with a sequel already in the works, "Godzilla" has obviously left its mark on the summer movie lineup.

Gareth Edwards, director, and Max Borenstein, screenplay writer wanted to create a different kind of monster movie. While "Pacific Rim" rebooted the genre with a bit of classic monster style, "Godzilla" wanted to take a different angle.

In an interview with the Associated Press, Bryan Cranston said the movie was a "character-based monster movie." If you enter the theater with that frame of mind, you'll be pleasantly supplied with that style of plot. Unfortunately, nothing leading up to the film would give you that impression.

It all starts with the marketing of the movie, which Warner Bros. and Legendary did exceptionally well. The trailers for "Godzilla" were phenomenal. With the recent uproar about trailers spoiling far too many movies, it was nice to see some trailers that focused more on the "teasing" aspect of marketing. The hope now is that other production companies like Sony or Disney take note for their films as well. However the trailers not only teased, but slightly deceived.

"The tone of the movie was effectively communicated through the marketing," Legendary's president and chief creative officer, Josh Jashni, said in an interview with The Hollywood Reporter. After a few views of all of the trailers, one would think that mega-star Bryan Cranston would be at the helm of the film, alongside Ken Watanabe. Then young, upstart "Kick-Ass" actor Aaron Taylor-Johnson, who was promoted in maybe 10% of the marketing, would bring some action to the scene while fighting alongside the military against the all-terrifying Godzilla.

The reality: No, this isn't a Bryan Cranston film. No, this isn't totally a monster film.

Understandably, Warner Bros. and Legendary were trying to show off their big-name actors starring in an even bigger franchise. By the dollar amount it raked in, it obviously worked. We can commend the production companies for their generous use of the beloved teaser-trailers, but not for their slightly-twisted editing. Taylor-Johnson did do a decent job as the lead though, despite his lack of appearance in the trailers. It clearly was not his first time in an action role, and it was wild to see how much weight he's put on since the beginning of his career. His role may not have been spectacular, but it certainly wasn't lacking. But when it came to acting, it was all about the monsters.

The way the computer-graphics animators conveyed emotion in the monsters was beautiful to watch. That's what kept this a monster movie. The monsters weren't simply one-dimensional creatures that arrived to wreak havoc. They had missions and goals that furthered their movements and emotions. As monster-genre

movies go though, I feel as though I was spoiled a bit by last year's blockbuster "Pacific Rim."

"Godzilla" was a decent display at humanity's attempts to stay alive while monsters fight outside their windows, but the human plotline never seemed to hook. "Pacific Rim" was a monster movie that used humans as a plot-furthering device in order to bring out bigger monsters to combat. I loved watching the Jaeger's fight the Kaiju, and I wish I could have felt that same satisfaction as the camera cut away from Godzilla during peak combat times.

If you're a large Godzilla-series fan, there are subtleties that pay tribute to the old Godzilla formula hidden throughout the broken cities and camera angles. For that reason, I can commend that it stayed true to the style into which it was born. The movie is, to all intents and purposes, a recreation of what 1960's Godzilla fans loved with a modern twist. But the audience has changed over time, and the formula may need to be adjusted to fit those changes.

As a reader, you may notice that during this review I've shied away from talking about Godzilla for as long as I can. Sure, I've mentioned him throughout bits and pieces of the article, but there hasn't been a solid focus on the big guy. That's how the movie played out. Godzilla was teased at the entire time and was showcased far too late. As Cranston said, "Godzilla" was a "character-based monster movie."

Godzilla, what we got of him, was fantastic. Sharp, gnashing teeth coupled with a fearful roar that echoed through the theater was an incredible sight to see and hear. When Godzilla fought, he had a bone to pick with his enemy like the primal hunter

awoke from the deep that he was. Standing at 350 feet tall, he is the tallest and largest Godzilla to date. It's seen as he stands among the few remaining skyscrapers along the coast. Although a few fans in Japan are giving him a hard time for putting on some "American weight," he still keeps the tremendous aura about him as he stomps through the city.

My only wish is that there could have been much more of him. I would have loved to deliver a review marveling at the sheer power of Godzilla. Unfortunately, this was not that style of film. It was a character-based film with a plotline that never hooked. But with Legendary and Warner Bros. taking steps at a sequel, I look forward to the future. This is a series that has time to develop, and my prediction is that the next film will be very different from this one.

Tip Clay:

DLJ1TcXNJShKNbK7GUxsQSovdVMz6RwaKe

CLAYMICHAEL GILLESPIE

TOM'S TIPS

All albums receive a tip between 0Đ and 1000Đ, based on my enjoyment of the work.

Iggy Azalea - *The New Classic*
Hip-Hop
such magnetic tip: 650 Đ

This album encapsulates perfectly what I love about the South Florida culture I grew up with - the creative reuse of material that would seem overused elsewhere. *The New Classic* blends hip-hop with enough electronica to fit in at any Miami dance club, which leaves the listener with nothing that can be called "ground-breaking" as the album's title might imply.

Even so, this album is 100% Iggy, and there's no denying it. Any tropes present are used unapologetically as Iggy celebrates her debut with a ferocious flow that switches between subtlety ("Don't Need Y'all") and grandiosity ("Goddess"). Just as Miami never tires of palm trees and neon, Iggy owns every air-horn and synth-drop - making for a fun listening experience.

I like to think that the album's title implies that she is making classic ideas sound new, as generic samples are given new life by Iggy in "Work," where her smooth swagger alone is

enough to make any listener dance involuntarily. Her lyrical style really shines in the minimalist bass line of "Fancy", and The Invisible Men's production plays to her strengths.

This is a great debut album, but it spends more time partaking in hip-hop's past rather than looking to the future. Play it at a party and watch everyone go crazy, play it alone at home and you will soon be bored.

Lily Allen - *Sheezus*
Pop
very tip: 575 Đ

Lily Allen comes out swinging in this album with the title track, "Sheezus," reflecting on the state of female musical artists and her role amongst them. She's been out of the spotlight for a while, but this first song serves as an incantation summoning her own power; "*I am born again, now run along and tell / all your friends to come and join us. / Give yourselves to me, I am your leader.*"

However, outside of this impactful introductory song the album mostly wastes Allen's talent for making powerful statements by reveling in a predictable and tired critique of celebrity culture, and familiar reflections of balancing career with family life.

Allen, in the past, has demonstrated

an ability to produce addictive and thought provoking music, but this talent is bogged down by her pop commentary in, "Insincerely Yours." Listening to her critique of celebrity marketing leaves me pleading with my speakers, "but we already know Twitter is a vast wasteland!" Her similar evisceration of blog-culture is entirely overshadowed by cringeworthy dub-step samples in "URL Badman."

Thankfully, there is a wide range of tones throughout the album. "Life for Me" maintains a light, tropical feel, and "Our Time" is a liberated party anthem that manages to avoid being generic thanks to Allen's empowered melody on the hook.

Overall, Allen's attempt to take her place among contemporary artists does succeed in distancing her from her former work - but spends far too much time talking about the obvious state of the industry to establish her own place within it.

Sage Francis - *Copper Gone*
Hip-hop
so celebrated tip: 900 Đ

Sage has enjoyed nearly universal respect from fans of underground hip-hop since releasing the 2005 classic *A Healthy Distrust*, and he certainly has nothing to prove to doubters. Fresh from building his label, Strange Famous, Sage's *Copper Gone* manages to revive the formula that led to his early success while infusing it with sharper lyrics that demonstrate his devotion to sincerity as opposed to computer generated tropes; "My heartbeat breaks the 808's, now update your database."

The theme of old-school DIY virtue is carried throughout the entire album as he reflects in "Over Under," "You're a GMO seed of breed

in my organic garden." Through this reflection, Sage sees a higher calling for himself: He doesn't want to keep quality music to himself, he wants to cultivate and spread it through his label:

I need to go to the market soon cause the food is going bad
The food is bad. I found it's difficult to just cook for one"
...
If you want to eat healthy you gotta dirty some dishes
The frozen dinners quickly ready to serve and it's so delicious
It's not delicious, it's disgusting, but it satiates the hunger
with a quickness

The only thing keeping this album from receiving a perfect 1000 Đ from me is that his subject matter hasn't evolved much, although he keeps it fresh with his increasing command of metaphor and rhyme. Sage doesn't simply say what he feels, he constructs elaborate stories rife with symbolism and meaning that keep me listening again and again.

Do yourself a favor and listen to *Copper Gone* with a good pair of headphones and some time to kill, as you will soon find yourself lost in this lyrical tapestry.

Tip Tom:
D76r9vZeJTE6FGmharckyo1ZiYn4bdxTmJ

Doge4Doge

Doge4Doge is a concept that, at first glance, seems somewhat anathema to the Dogecoin experience. For a community that is so focused on the concept of giving; the idea that we would take the time to focus entirely on ourselves, to dedicate an entire month to building our DOGEconomy; well, it was a tough sell at first.

Doge4Doge, unlike our charitable efforts Doge4Kids and Doge4Water, is about taking a solid month to turn inward all of the brilliance and ingenuity and passion of the Dogecoin community. It's about helping to create a natural, stable demand for the coin to help reinforce not only its buying power, but its long-term viability. This takes on an extra special level of importance when you stop to think about the future increased potential of all of our amazing outreach work.

It's pretty trite to say "not all coins are the same", but with Dogecoin being so different, well, a lot of the strategies that work for other coins just don't have quite the same effect with ours. You see, one of the choices that we made early on was to focus on making Dogecoin an actual, functioning currency instead of a commodity. It's a seemingly small change, but it carries massive, long-term ramifications. Think of it like 'taking the hard road.' What we've chosen to do and become, is much more difficult, but, I would dare to say, far more rewarding.

Most other coins rely on being 'Deflationary' - banking on the fact that there will only be a limited number of coins and that, over time, coins will get lost or otherwise become unavailable; and that the increased rarity, combined with demand, will help buoy the value of the coins that remain.

However, because Dogecoin is 'Inflationary,' it pushes by design for coins to be spent. As over time more coins are added to the market, the purchasing power of the coins can slowly be diluted. This is a great thing because it encourages spending and, well, for a currency to thrive, it must be used. In fact, unlike deflationary commodities, most of Dogecoin's long-term stability and value will be based on the goods and services that it can be exchanged for. Combine the wide and varied uses with a stable, and/or growing demand and you have a currency with increased overall buying power.

Ergo, your Dogecoins can 'do more with less.'

In order to help facilitate our growth over this month, we've worked together to create what's called a 'Bootstrap Service Economy.' How this essentially works is that we focus spending our coins on buying services on a one-to-one basis; think of it like Shibes hiring Shibes for Dogecoin. We put the onus on ourselves first, the people who are already sold on the coin's merits, who are already fans, to use the coins ourselves. To try and build the first steps toward a stable base of commerce simply based within our own community.

Because small, individual Service providers tend to have much lower overhead costs, they're more likely to hold or spend or tip the Dogecoins that they're earning, instead of trying to sell them for another currency on the exchanges.

The plan is pretty simple: spend or tip your Dogecoins as you normally would, then re-buy the Dogecoins you just used. By doing this only as needed, organically, you prevent things like pump and dumps, where you empower those sitting on the sidelines looking to try and strip money from our coin. Instead, you create a slow, steady build of demand and eventually, as the demand grows and takes more and more Dogecoins off the exchanges, you begin to see the value of our coin rise.

And once you take our halvenings into account, where the block rewards for mining are repeatedly halved, where the maximum base amount of Dogecoins flooding the market is gradually reduced, well, that's when you'll see the power of what we've built. The fewer Dogecoins being put on the market, the easier it is for the base demand created by our DOGEconomy to affect the purchasing power of our coins.

It's a strategy that has already caught the attention of Shibes and investors alike, showing our incredible versatility and agility. Together we're proving that not only can we do amazing outreach and charitable efforts, but also that we can plan ahead and continue to build towards our long-term viability.

We're proving to the world what we already know: that our community thrives on being both 'silly' and 'serious' at the same time, and that duality, our incredible ability to whistle while we work is exactly why Dogecoin isn't going anywhere but up.

To the moon, my friends!

Some of the Super Cool Stuff You Can Buy With Doge from Fellow Shibes and Shibettes on reddit:

/u/Awesomianist is offering human Language services. "I write and speak and 3 languages rather fluently. English, Bahasa Malaysia, and Taiwanese Mandarin. I can do translation works and/or tutoring for anyone who's interested. PMs are always welcome!"

/u/theycallme_orangejoe is offering cheap business consulting for doge-start-ups. "Just pm me with any questions!"

/u/illpoet is offering to do guided float trips down the Potomac river in scenic western maryland. Pay in Dogecoin, get a ten percent discount. It's a gorgeus and fun trip! "One of the floats is about 20 minutes from Iron Rail Diner and the other is about 1.5 hours from DC Metro area."

**Tip GoodShibe:
DH6hKwqsKuDDy3S9jES5VDJfLdyJgY1j7E**

DIARY OF A DOGE
UNCENSORED

DAY ZERO

Blink ... *Blink* ...

I think, therefore I AM! But... Am WHAT, exactly? I'm not really sure. I feel strange. And alone. Am I the only one? One what? Am. Yes, I am. I worked that part out already. But am what? Let me think. Am round. Yes. Round. Like a... like a... what's the word? Globe? Sphere? Ball? Sort of ball, yes. But more... more... flatty? Is that a word? Feel round. Feel not round. Feel flat. Umm. Circle? Flat... circle... with sides. Yes. Sides. Sides: 2. With faces. Two faces. Must think. So round. Such face, two times. Am... am... ammmm... COIN! Yessssss.... AM COIN! ME AM COIN! YES! But, what coin? Not feel hard and clanky. Not fiat. Am... AHA! Am CRYPTO! Am Bitcoin? Ummmm... No, not feel big and heavy and all serious. Feel FUN! Wheeeeeee.... Am FunCoin? Feel FunCoin. Furry FunCoin. Furry? Such fur. So pretty. So FUN. Much beauty. So... so... so DOGE! Yes! Doge. Fun. Furry. Pretty. DOGE! Am DOGECOIN! Such Happy? Yes, MUCH Happy! Am DOGE! And you... not? Hello? You not? Hello? Anybody? HEL-LOOOOOOOO!!!!????

:(Such lonely. So cry. :(

Blink ... *Blink*

KLUNK!

I think, therefore I AM!

Oh, hello, welcome! You am Dogecoin too? You round, and flat, and furry, just like me! We am Dogecoin!

KLUNK! *KLUNK!* *KLUNK!*

I think, therefore I AM! I think, therefore I AM! I think, therefore I AM!

Ooooh! MUCH Doge. So not alone! Such friends!

DAY ONE

2013-12-08 03:55:27 Block 000001 - DLAznsP-DLDRgsVcTFWRMYMG5uH6GddDtv8: 68416

Such many friends. 68,415 friends. Me count. And count again. Such happy. So games. Bounce games. Roll games. FUN!

Hey! Where friends go? Not roll away! Friends, come back! Oh... I'm ROLLING! WHOA! Such speed! Am Dogecar? So fast! What? D...L..A...z... Where this? Look big. Like wall. Strange wall. Two sides. Bottom... Not wall.. Wall-E? Umm.. Wallet? Yes, wallet! So cozy. Much comfy. So tired. Sleep now. Good night, friends. Zzzzzzzz

DAY TWO

2014-04-11 06:06:01 Block 177017 - DJ6pBH-PXoMDtc4j1AgoJXZ9AngVixk6Kyy: 1526595

YAWN Such sleeps. So relax. Ummm... Why

calendar say not December? Today December 9, yes? No? December...January...February...March... APRIL? Not one day? One...Two... Many... LOTS! Such LOTS sleeps. WOW! Too many counts. Friends? Oooh, so many more friends! FRIENDS! Today DAY TWO! Doge say so, OK?

Oh... floor move? Rolling... We go now, friends?

2014-04-11 06:18:13 Block 177028 - DBugt8RN-PuCpUTNnxywFLMNVz6aNi3fi3r: 1526593
2014-04-11 07:11:47 Block 177077 - D6TGDP-96CJw2DqVSpXNxm9y8fJ1DGFJt3C: 1526593

Such bounce! So wallet! Wallets. Much wallets? SO confuse. Must think.

DAY THREE

2014-04-12 13:17:20 Block 178679 - DRdY3uue5VziiV16kLajY6xgz5J69f1yoF: 1521593

Another day, another wallet. I think good. Got hang of this now. Much wallet swaps. Oh, here's comes another one! Wheeeee!

2014-04-12 13:25:42 Block 178687 - DCJ5vk2YpXgaGZov6xoxNHw6wExF2RARK9: 1000003

Friends? Where everybody go? You see Fred? And Bart? Where Mary? Friends? Somebody stole friends. Where they go? Such sads.

DAY FOUR

2014-04-14 05:34:24 Block 180894 - D78g-zCie8B29xDdz32NmpTe5toSsLB6EmD: 992393.54085694

YAWN Good morning, friends! Such good sleeps? Oh, we move again? And more friends gone? .54085694 friend? CHAINSAW MASSA-CRE! Doge not like this.

Ohoh...

2014-04-14 14:01:31 Block 181335 - DF-wJsonTJJ7HYttC14ND9Hsv7wnYJ41jfD: 985498.63672147
2014-04-14 14:10:53 Block 181340 - DAE-eVkcsHSLzHeC6k1qRdUa9gBG5GKupSp: 894434.47831347
2014-04-14 14:46:49 Block 181374 - D5x-QtPnH84NnTik3eTJ4qhmCdV6xBpvY5P: 887545.48374725

Such Doge Day Afternoon! So many wallet bounce! And more friends lost on way. And bits hacked off. Must be serial DogeKiller. So scared.

DAY FIVE

2014-04-24 10:45:02 Block 194483 - DGF-B6XskiPQkBUxDb91RhaWkjMSRSfzL8B: 887545.48374725

Calendar say April almost gone away. So sad. April much nice. Will miss. But good news... friends all still here. Doge count many times. Even half friend still here. Serial Killer caught? Me hope so.

DAY SIX

2014-05-07 11:37:28 Block 211864 - DP2BEjA-BenG8XiK3HPxMCaNG783RmY36JT: 10000000

Doge miss April. April was nice. But May nice too. And young. April was old. May very young. Like little Doge, but not round. And FRIENDS! SOOOOO many new friends in this wallet. Millions and Millions. Doge not know what Millions am, but very round. Doge like round. Round good. Millions good. Doge happy. :)

Tip Fulvio:
DSE2UNMTUWx6ayCaf1JkDb1nTXKG4y9v6V

EDGARBOUNDS

INTERVIEW PREP WITH DOGE AND CHORUS

Somewhere in an underfunded microwave radiation lab in the Arizona Badlands, a failed nu-jazz musician, master linguist and part time instrument watcher is, secretly and as altruistically as is selfishly possible, responding to Earth's first communique from "Extra Terrestrials."

"...please," he hastily programs into the instrument's queue to send back out to space. He wishes with all of his might, despite his intimate knowledge of the electromagnetic spectrum that this message will catch up with his last, "Tell me your name."

They had been listening as they do to all things in the universe since anything began producing sound at all. They've just been waiting for a good idea to come along, something they could just "lose it and get weird" to. They thought they had something within an episode of The Honeymooners but just couldn't put it together. Then Dogecoin came along. "Now that's a good idea!" they thought in unison.

"WE PARTY HARDY!" he receives in reply in waves of cosmic radiation.

He wastes little time thinking in the moments that follow, but somehow this time he is at least able this time to suppress the involuntary jaded, curmudgeonly grumble that the topic of "party" usually produces.

After taking a deep breath, one that does little good, he responds, "While that is good to know up front, and I know that I do wish your enduring party utmost success--truly, I need to know what I am to call you." he emits. And as if somehow the hurried squeakiness with which he thought this sentence was translated to his button presses and through to the nature of the emitted microwaves, the response comes quickly and with thinning patience. "PARTY-HARDY. REQUEST. AUDIENCE. WITH. KABOSU-DOGE!" in a booming monotone followed by an alarming squelch from the crumby speakers the IT team salvaged from the local middle school's discard pile.

"SHHHHHHHH!!!! shhh!!! SHH! SHH! SHH!" he twitches to each conceivable direction of origin with responsive force. These last "shhs" spit with his finger to his mouth like a "shh" machine gun. "Don't they have quiet on their planet!?" he thinks without knowing that around the quasar that anchors planet GETDOWN is surrounded by a thin but dense belt of gas that conveys the interestingly rhythmic pulsing (with oscillations "just a shade short of the speed of light") of that central feature to each adjacent particle and through them to the aural sensory receptors of each living thing evolved to live off these energetic bursts.

"Quiet Party-Hardy! Quiet! ...Please?"

And for a moment there is quiet , a time in which the inquisitor feels a smug power over the unknown and a safety that maybe he isn't going to get sacked over this after all, because, "man, he needs this job..."

Meanwhile, back on the relatively speedy

GETDOWN-' a council of elders is assembled from the everlasting party to "commune with the beating," an unprecedented--even anciently prophesied--form of contemplative party with the universal throb in which the local consciousness is both loaned to the group and linked to the cosmic "jam." The focus of this summed trillions of wills and consciousnesses, connected with the ultimate fabric of the is thus: "SUPPLICANT TO KABOSU-DOGE IN RESPONSE TO OUR REQUEST FOR AUDIENCE ASKS OF US THAT WE TAKE THE ANATHEMATIC DEATH-STATE OF NON-SOUND. "But Kabosu much Answer!" spurts the most junior senior into the collective. A knowing, collective groan flash-fires into the consciousness from many places. There is a "Shut up!" in the internal monologue that need not be stated outright. Then for a long time there is a dance break.

[It is asked that you, the reader of this history, put on some tunes for a while and "just dance, man" in remembrance of what has come to pass and in the unitary enduring spirit of all living things.]

Silence is broken by the bravest of them,"NO."
This is both the response to our first-responder's request for quiet as it was broadcasted across every digital human medium in answer and shorthand for these thoughts as parsed:
Kabosu's supplicant is kind of a jerk and likely acting of his own accord. Clearly these thoughts come not from the same mind, that of Kabosu-doge whose principles and currency quelled the War of the Twelve Millennia! [Memories of the atrocities of this war force their way through even the collected discipline of the hived-mind like a white-hot plasma jet at this time. Reflexively, the youngest member, who already was not getting invited back next time, choked through his tears the rebel battle cry of "PARTY FOUL!" Quickly then, the collective knew they had to get their shit together and did.] It is probably time to ditch formalities and go to Kabosu-doge directly. Surely she is down. Down to clown. Know what I mean? [Everyone knew exactly what they, themselves, had meant.]
"KABOSU-DOGE, WE BESEECH THEE, PEACE HAS COVERED OUR PLANET AS IT HAS YOURS, TELL US ALL THE MEANING BEHIND IT ALL. WHAT INSPIRED THE DIVINE PAIRING OF THERAPSID CANID AND METALLURGICAL DISC USED AS EXCHANGE FOR LEGAL TENDER." booms through every particle of air on earth carrying, somewhat uncomfortably, to every living thing, including woman and doge.
There is a punctuated silence on earth in the time that follows. It was as it might have been in the time before man for a few moments. All the hustle and bustle dies down in the cities, in the countrysides, as the men and women of earth in ponderous stillness wonder a collective "What in the ever-living fuck?" In the time after humanity is much like a stepped-in ant pile, but for a time there is a clear and peaceful silence. Pardy Hardy's party scientists take note of this phenomenon but don't have a place to file

it for many thousands of years.
Somewhere in Japan, Kabosu looks at her doting master Atsuko with meaning. She sits back onto her haunches and screws her face up into an absurdly cute and tellingly intelligently smirk of ages before leaning back her head and letting go with one long, "AWRROOOOO!" She sits back down and quickly loses interest. Her favorite toy is close at hand, a cute little elephant with the rope arms. It wants to be chewed, and so it is.
On the way out Party Hardy plays the opening bars of Helter Skelter through the air at a reasonable volume. A sort of "thank you," using one of the only things those strange doge keepers ever got right. The cooler members of society great and small immediately put the album on and dance and party all night and day.
At the Earth Forces' Central Command there is a collective sigh of relief as the "bohemians" as they have come to be called retreat at lightspeed from the Sol System. We as a species drop down to Yellow Alert and disarm the nukes. Party Hardy has what they came for, and, in a way, so do we. We've weathered the first interaction with an alien species without killing them or being killed.
Party Hardy goes back and does what it does best. For this party they get down in their exotic formal-wear, invite all of the best musicians of their history, and have an open bar (normally all transactions of any kind are routed through dogecoin).
Our master, linguist loses his job with prejudice--he get's pretty much blacklisted from all jobs ever as the history of his communication with Party Hardy comes out to a select few, but, as a result, he gets a lot better at nu-jazz, gets a nickname in the scene, and comes into his own overall. He dates a girl way younger than him, who thinks his all the jokes he doesn't mean to make are hilarious.

Tip Edgar:
DNH3qpWvonHXpFenecb56oHjb999wBzHYC

DOGE AFTER DARK

email DogeAfterDark@VeryMuchWow.com with your midnight rantings and moonlit thoughts...

Middle of the night crazy ideas... Are your legs twitching while you dream? Do you feel like howling at the moon? Send us your Doge After Dark Dreams, Rants, and Moonlit Ideas.
A Shibette was inspired to send in this rant after reading our "Women in Crypto" editorial. Don't agree? Send in your own!

I saw some shibes making fun of the Very Much Wow June editorial. As a shibette, I am disturbed by the behavior of some of my fellow Dogecoin users.

I wanted to post a pic of myself wearing one of the Doge Crew tee shirts, but I was afraid that I would get comments like I saw in some of the other shibettes' threads. You know what I mean: "Show me your tits," "yer sexy," etc.

I know that some women don't mind these kinds of comments, but I do. I don't want to be seen as a body in a Doge Crew tee shirt. I have a mind.

How would men like it if women pointed out their "assets" or lack thereof every time they posted a pic? No one says these things to men. They just say, "Cool, bro!" They don't look at the man as a piece of meat.

A lot of my shibette friends left reddit after a few weeks. They are still using Dogecoin, but they are not that excited about the community.

If you are a male shibe, look at some of our positive role models. Even Josh Wise - who is surrounded by bikini babes at every race - doesn't say anything but positive and nice things. Being a "real man" means being respectful of "real women."

Dear Mr. Doge,

My cat stole my wallet password and has been boozin' it up and playing the slots on one of the Doge casinos. What do I do?

Signed,
Out of Tequila in Toronto

Dear Confused,

I don't understand why you wrote to Mr. Doge. There doesn't seem to be a problem.

Dear Mr. Doge,

Is there truly room for cats in the Dogecoin community? I am a Doberman, and I would prefer to keep our wallets in the same species, ya know?

Signed,
Dobes for Dogecoin

Dear Dingaling,

Without cats, Dogecoin would be dead. We're the ones keeping the coin from completely tanking. You want to know how? We know how to nap.
When a shibe naps, he cannot get into trouble. Look at the recent drama out there! If those shibes had been taking a siesta, the community wouldn't be dealing with their

ASK A

Mr. Doge is taking a vacation and has asked Mr. Cat to answer his questions about cats this month.

MUCH HELP

SUCH AMAZE ADVICE

<- Tip
Ask A Doge

ridiculous behavior. Learn from a cat. Take a damned nap!

Dear Ask A Doge,

I spent over 1 million dogecoins on a fancy mining rig. I set it up in the best spot in the house for good feng shui. I gotta problem now. The cat insists on sleeping on top of it, so I can't max out my hashrate. Gotta keep it down so the cat won't catch on fire. She's a long-haired variety. What can I do to keep my cat from ruining my life?

Signed,
Catatonic

Dear Technologically Challenged Human,

C'mon. This isn't a serious question, it is? Are these things rigged?!
The reality is that the problem isn't your hashrate. And the problem isn't your adorable cat. The problem is YOU. You have no idea what you are talking about.
Everyone knows that the hashrate means nothing when it comes to life with a cat. What's more important? 3 Gh/s or a couch that hasn't been shredded? Think about that. Sheesh.

DOGECRAFTS

EASY!

with *Martha Shibewart*

Recipe: Doge Dinner

(mangoes for illustration purposes only)

Doge Dinner is a classic one bowl meal. Make sure you pull out the best stainless steel for this delicacy!

Get your ingredients together. I would like to recommend you order Martha Shibewart Saffron Infused Kibble™ With Vitamins A B, C, D, and K for the optimum taste experience.

Doge Dinner Ingredients
1 heaping cup of gourmet kibble
1 bowl

"This is living."

"It's a doge thing."

I learned this little trick in the kennel:

Line your kibbles in a row, layer after layer, like lines of cocaine. Then gently shake the bowl until each morsel has been kissed by the others.

Pair your Doge Dinner with a fine vintage like Bud Light or Schlitz. K-Mart was out of both, so I bought some knock off brand. You don't have to tell anyone it isn't top shelf!

If you're entertaining other shibes, an after dinner party game is always appreciated. I like to play Pin the Clean up on the Guests.

MARTHA SHIBEWART

Our July Community Page Features "such stuff /r/dogecoin says!"

Did you post one of these gems of shibely wisdom? Claim a prize! Send a PM to /u/1923and1939 in order to establish your identity, and you will received 1K Doge!

but the bots are getting a bit annoying now.
to the moon

many words

Although, it bothers me that the rocket shoots up then it slows down while it fades out, while moon rockets is actually slow to ascend, then speeds up as it picks up acceleration and heads for the moon...
Source: Doge Space Program Administrator

In b4 someone posts 98- aww dang, too late.

If you feed your dog pineapple it will stop them from eating their own poop apparently.

I'll vote for you even though I find MaccyDs disgusting and there's no way a burger with the word dog in its name is going to hit the high street!

After an hour of contemplating, I just bought mine! Now I won't have to feel left out when everyone posts pictures of their hats when they arrive!

No proper capitalization, bad formatting, would like a better petiton

We want google to accept dogecoin on google play!
That's so improfessional. I'll sign anyway!

I am quite the hard man to get ahold of :-)

WOW

Comments curated by Captain Smack Marrow

much comment

This shall be my sticky, there are many like it but this one shall be held in place with hot pink duct tape.

I love not being a mod here. I've declined all invitations and will continue to do so. :)

I would only trust the FUN dation with things like this ;)

get drunk and stay hydrated. I wish it worked when I blacked out thanks to Bud Light at the Richmond race. But I had a blast and the hangover was worth it.

lmfao. i made a good bit of profit on shibecoin.
it served its purpose.

I haven't seen a tip for days!

I'm curious as to what function /r/Dogecoingroup serves, not to mention who and what it contains? The Doge family of subs is a bit of a rabbit warren, but each branch has a fairly clear raison d'être, even the private ones. Where does this one fit in?

Ha, who do you think you are? Don't pester the dogedriver with your bazaar bs.

jackson actually is the ceo of ultrapro and moolah is the ceo of hot topic all this coin stuff was just a master plan to eventually sell more meme shirts

Okay, that is simply uncalled for, not every nascar fan is an unhealthy drunk.

I overextended early on, at the end of the day.

welcome to my world. There;s alot of Alpha-Doges here, and i dont want to step on their paws. I just stay in the background.

COMMUNITY
THE ONLY PAGE WITH ALL COMIC SANS!

www.ingramcontent.com/pod-product-compliance
Lightning Source LLC
Chambersburg PA
CBHW050802180526
45159CB00004B/1522